He Called Me Commander

Joyce Strahn

BALBOA
PRESS
A DIVISION OF HAY HOUSE

Balboa Press books may be ordered through booksellers or by contacting:

Balboa Press
A Division of Hay House
1663 Liberty Drive
Bloomington, IN 47403
www.balboapress.com
1-(877) 407-4847

ISBN: 978-1-4525-4913-2 (sc)
ISBN: 978-1-4525-4912-5 (e)

Library of Congress Control Number: 2012905701

Printed in the United States of America

Balboa Press rev. date: 04/02/2012

DEDICATION

This book is lovingly dedicated to Gayl Fraser who channeled the information from my space family and friends and from whom I have learned so much on my spiritual journey; to Johnathan Hammer who channeled the information on Arcturus and the Aaschjan; to Susan Leland from www.ashtarontheroad.com for channeling the reading with Ashtar himself; to Jeannie Parker who gave me permission to use her transcription from Hatonn; to my friend, Tenaso from Americus aka Tennie Bottomly with whom I have walked in so many lifetimes; to my Arcturian shipmates who shared my home on and off for a period of over three years; and to my very personal friends Ashtar, Sananda, St. Germain, and Archangel Michael with whom I have walked many, many times. So many thanks to all of you.

Table of Contents

Introduction

If this book has found its way into your hands, you have a deep Knowing that there is more to this life than what you have been led to believe by those who control our media and our governments. It has taken me twenty five years to be ready to release this material, and I have painstakingly transcribed it word for word from very poor quality tapes, because I believe it is so important to get this information out now when contact from other life planes is so eminent.

I have been studying and teaching the Divine Mysteries for more than thirty years, and if there is one thing that I have learned, it is that it is all God. It is all Divine. Whether the life sources are on another planet, another star, or within the Earth—whether they are plants, animals, devas, cetaceans, Mother Gaia herself—it is all Divine. We are all from the same Source. We all share the same life force.

Our people have been conditioned into believing that those who come from space are "bad guys" and are coming to destroy us. It's everywhere—in our controlled media, the games our kids play, the movies, television—all of these are ploys to control us by fear—the trump card the Illuminati have used to control us for hundreds of years.

Anyone who has had first hand knowledge of these occurrences has had his/her credibility destroyed, and even though the evidences from ancient pyramids and pictographs on stone to crop circles and physical remains of crashed vehicles are right in front of us, we are made to believe that all of this is a hoax and a figment of our imaginations.

I do not buy into any of the "approved" media responses. Fox News and similar sources are not welcome in my home, nor do I allow movies and media of any kind that promotes violence to enter my "computer", my brain, because those pictures find a way to control and condition my thinking, and I know none of it is true. The experiences I have had with Ashtar and Sananda and all of those in the material in this book are so personal and the energy so intense, that there is no mistaking that what I am presenting is the Truth.

For more than 36 years, I have been a real estate broker in Bozeman, Montana, where I owned my own office, and in Salem, Oregon. I am known for my complete honesty, my straight thinking, and my integrity . . . so for me to present material that is anything less than absolute Truth is unthinkable. I was raised on an Iowa farm where a handshake and your word were your calling cards, and I can assure you, that this material is no less than that.

But, I will tell you this—in order for you to take this in—knowing the conditioning you have had on this plane, it will be very important for you keep an open mind and an open heart as you read this material, to breathe often, and to surround yourself with white Light. For some of you it will not be easy to hear; for others, it will be the revelation you have been waiting for.

So . . . let us begin.

My Story

On July 28, 1981, I was gifted with a set of books called "The Course in Miracles", 1188 pages of extremely difficult material that I suspected at the time was an update of what we know as the Bible. Just recently, it has been confirmed to me by Ashtar, that Sananda gave this gift to the world, and it was just that. The introduction of it says:

> *"This is a course in miracles. It is a required course. Only the time you take it is voluntary. Free will does not mean that you can establish the curriculum. It means only that you can elect what you want to take at a given time. The course does not aim at teaching the meaning of love, for that is beyond what can be taught. It does aim, however, at removing the blocks to the awareness of love's presence, which is your natural inheritance. The opposite of love is fear, but what is all-encompassing can have no opposite.*

> *This course can therefore be summed up very simply in this way:*

> **Nothing real can be threatened.**
> **Nothing unreal exists.**

> *Herein lies the peace of God.*

The Course in Miracles
Copyright 1975 by the Foundation for Inner Peace.

Within a short time after receiving this "gift", a class of 24 people came together in Bozeman, Montana, to study it. I felt such power from this material that I simply lifted sentences and made fill-in-the-blank discussion material. We did all three of the books at the same time.

When after a year of intense study, we completed the work, we began it again, and in that second year, we were led to two very wonderful channels, Dayana Jon Patterson channeling AMAG, and Gayl Kellenberger through whom the material in this book was channeled. I cannot tell you how grateful and how honored I am to have had this opportunity in this lifetime. It was truly the opening to a lifetime of study and enlightenment, and some of those who shared that experience with me are still very dear friends.

For three years, at least once a week and sometimes as many as three times a week, groups of us studied with these channels and were introduced to the Divine on many levels. I remember distinctly the cold Montana night when Gayl channeled what she had described as "The Far Stars". We had been told this would be the program for that night because there were many from different planets and star systems wanting so much to let us know they were here. When she channeled the Arcturians, I KNEW that was where I came from. There was no mistaking the energy that correlated with mine.

I went outside when the channeling was complete and looked up into the star filled, cold, clear night. At that time, I was struggling to keep my real estate office afloat in another downturn in the market. I had seen a large painting in a gallery in Maui a short time before that depicted a knight in full armor on a white horse on a field of ice. All four of the horse's legs were chained to the ground and there was no way, he could make headway on the ice. Far in the distance in the clouds, there were more knights coming to help and this described what I knew to be true, that we earthlings would get help from our brothers and sisters in space. I remember calling out in a very loud voice to that night sky, "Where in the name of heaven have you been?"

In 1986, I could not longer keep my office together, so I left Montana and came to Oregon where the downturn in the market had bottomed out and I could start over. Gayl would make many trips to Oregon and channel to various groups in towns here and she always stayed at my house. This story begins in 1987 when she became the first conduit that my Arcturian shipmates could communicate through as they attempted to study me and learn how to live on planet Earth. It was to be the beginning of another exciting time.

And so we continue to wait—though now the time is very short and help is already in place. The twenty five years I have studied need to be distilled into three, the extension of time we have been given, as Mother Gaia will have completely ascended into the 5th Dimension by 2015, so it is time now for me to release this material.

Recent scientific releases tell us there are probably thousands of planets, and other Higher sources that I consider to be even more valid say that many of these planets and stars contain life.

If you will, please bring through the crown chakra at the top of your head the white Christ Light and SEE it swirling across your body to the right and to the left and swirling around and back and up and out through your entire auric system. Do this each time you pick up this material and KNOW in your hearts of hearts that it comes to you from the very highest of Sources and will open you to the possibilities of the life that abounds in this Universe.

Hang on. You are in for a great ride!

Joyce Strahn

Chapter 1

He Called Me Commander

"The breeze at dawn has secrets to tell you
Don't go back to sleep!
You must ask for what you really want.
Don't go back to sleep!
People are going back and forth across the doorsill where the two
worlds touch.
The door is round and open.
Don't go back to sleep!"

From the Chinook

It was January, 1987, six months after I had moved to Salem, Oregon, to start my real estate career over again.

I was at a very low period of my life. The real estate market had crashed in Montana. I had left my beautiful home there, my office that I had started and groomed and held together by my fingertips, one son who was still in college at Montana State, and my spiritual bases—everything was gone.

There I had been President of my Unity Church, President of the Board of Realtors and had friends and family and a State that I truly loved. The money that I had brought with me had long since gone and I had had to

1

sell most of my furniture to even keep going. It takes a long time to get started in real estate, especially when you don't know any one or anything about the area, and I was forty seven years old. Also, I was about to go to my bankruptcy hearing. From my childhood, there was no greater shame than bankruptcy.

This was the energy that my channel friend, Gayl, came into when she arrived to stay at my apartment on her rounds of doing sessions in several Oregon towns. I wanted to take her around and show her some of beautiful Oregon, so we made our way to Silver Falls State Park, a magnificent park about 30 miles east of Salem.

We had not even left the car and she said, "Archangel Michael is here. He wants to talk to you." The following is directly from that transcript:

Archangel Michael speaks—We have erected a tower at the lake (Hidden Lake where I was living) and Ashtar will begin to speak to you there right after the bankruptcy hearing.

I am Michael. I thought I would like to look around here a little bit. I have never seen such a forest as this.

"Oh, this is beautiful!"

When you step out of the car, stretch yourself tall and remember that you are Captain Haelegram of the Arcturus fleet. Remember that. And you are a very small female here. You were a very large male on Arcturus, so go to that energy. It is you. You are doing what you need to do. You are acting on the precepts of your reality. It is unrealistic to try to carry a steamship, but you can carry a canoe. So, we are going to get you a canoe.

So . . . I am Michael and I am with you every moment. You must remember that. You are getting scared sometimes. *You are here on temporary assignment. You are on loan from the Universe.* And remember that. When it is abundantly fearsome, say. "Well, I knew that it wouldn't always be a picnic, and I knew that there would be scary days, and I know, too, that it is paying off. It is working."

This is reality. The abundance of those beyond and how they perceive this action, how they perceive the force of energy upon the earth, that is what you are speaking of. The ones beyond know what is happening. They see it. They see the change. The abundance of revelation in the hearts and minds of the people on the planet is truly astonishing! I tell you it is much more than we expected! And how do you think this would have happened if you hadn't been here, you and the others? How do you think this would have happened?

"I don't know."

It would not! Hmmph! It would not. So give yourself credit. Stand right up in front of your mirror every morning and say, "I know what I am."

You are not alone. Many are coming around you. Be in your modes with them sometimes doing the work seriously, but remember there is Light play. Go to things with these people and laugh. Do not let seriousness be a part of your life. We can say this is a serious endeavor, but immediately, we must make a joke. That is the way it is in the Universe. The Universe has not a serious bone in its body. Truly. It is more in abundant clarity of the joy always shining. And if that is the way of joking, that is the way of laughing, then that is the expression. If it is just contentment, that is another way. If it is music, that is another way. Perhaps with your music, you can get New Age songs going and play and play.

So, all right, remember that I am here, BC (Michael often refers to Sananda as Brother Christ) is here and you are here. And you are not going with us, we are going with you. We are following you. Remember, you have led. So, there is no fear whatsoever.

We have no fear for you. That is not even called faith. It is called trusting. It is called trusting your comrades, trusting your compatriots of the Universal Legions. When you move through this time, you will remember far more than you could ever imagine. So, don't try to devise how you will see, because you cannot even imagine how you will see. It will be far more than you could devise.

3

Now, I completely remove myself from this form. Although she knows that I am in accord of her vibration, she needs a little sustaining energy to balance.

Do you know that I can be with you at all times? Are you aware of this, that Michael vibration can be called into your form at all times?

"I do it sometimes with the flame." (The violet flame.)

It is up to you. You see, BC is with you whether you want it or not—that is kind of a Universal joke—

"I try not to impose on you."

BC is with you whether you like it or not, but Michael can be but by request. It is my function, also, and it is not an imposition, it is an availability of energy. I can be a component of your energy at all times. It helps you focus, but fire rather than any kind of rankle. There is a difference. Spiritual fire is wonderful. I love spiritual fire.

OK. OK. I am going now from her form, but I do want to make it clear to you. I am in abundance.

"I am glad things are going well with all of what we are doing."

Oh, very, very well. It takes a high note of cheer to keep that kind of energy going, and that is why we want you laughing a lot because otherwise you would get too tired and bogged down. And, that is why we are helping you, because it helps the energy flow at a different level. It is to maintain this pace that we will be doing for the next few years will be quite a challenge. It is hard, but it can be done.

"Thank you."

The next morning Gayl came out of the shower laughing. "I stepped into your shower and this man's voice started talking to me. He said, 'These are Joyce's things. What are you doing using Joyce's things?' I started communicating with him and he told me his name was Aleckatron and he was from Arcturus and that he was a scientist who built geodesic domes on Arcturus. He said a contingent of them were here in your house because you and they are from the same starship and they are learning from you how to live in Earth energy."

I was not surprised, just delighted that I could be of service to them. So . . . that evening we did a channeling and Aleckatron came through for the first time.

Aleckatron's First Visit

I have a mode that is different from yours. I am trying to make adjustment to the light flow.

"Do you want me to turn that off?"

No, it is all right. I am doing this. It is with my energy level that I must come into better coordination. I must learn these things. It is an important part of what I will be doing here.

As you have been abundantly made clear to, I am called Aleckatron. I am one of the dominion of Arcturus, as you are, also. I am having a novice training in the respects of living in a town on the planet called Earth. I have not been a novice in any other way. It is an interesting experience to be called upon to attempt this sort of endeavor. I have not been asked to do this anywhere, anytime before now. As I have become accustomed to your space in this State called Oregon and in this planet called Earth, I have come now from the place called Silver Falls where my colony does abide, as does yours.

I have not been so long upon this place called planet Earth, but since I have been in your way as your advisor and counselor, although you do not know it so well as exactly you will know it from now on. I have made abundant adjustments now in my energy flow as the establishment of the energy upon the planet is required to be in gradients of what is esteemed to be normal upon the planet Arcturus. There are gradients to infuse more energy to withstand and gradients to diffuse energy, to become subtler and then pass to and fro. This is a difficult challenge for those of us who have been here such a short time.

There is an abundance of energy in the place called "sleeping room" with the help of others from the colony. We have magnified the intensification of habitable energy for us. Thus, you can be accorded into the dignity of your home space, also, when you are in your sleeping space because you now have Arcturian energy focalization in the place of your sleeping. Do not think that it is abundantly exactly the same as Arcturus. It is still somewhat immobilized by the planet Earth vibrations as well as those vibrations of the town you dwell in. But . . .

Though I bid thee welcome. I do know of your ways. Yes, I am an engineer, also.

Channel's husband enters the room—"Oh, is that right?"

Yes, I have been upon the planet Arcturus since the beginning of my days. I have not traveled much being of inordinate scientific nature. I then sounded out a pattern for myself upon the scanner and found that I was led to this position upon Earth at this time. Having coordinated with a former shipmate, I then could in sequence come into being here. It is not such a focalization of energy as you may know as form, but similar in that I have frequently contributed my form cellular structure into this pattern.

If you could say of your forms in a scientific manner, in an engineering manner, that you could take out of a certain group of cells, let us use numbers of ten, and they represent an area, a certain frequency, a certain dimension in the form that you inhabit, a certain function. If for instance, in the crudest analysis, you were to say let us take one cell out of ten, and create a pattern that is clearly form but not so intensive. This is what I have done.

Channel's husband—"Is this different from being in Spirit? Is being in the etheric different?"

Very different.

Channel's husband—"How? How can you explain that to us?"

Etheric is as your programming is inherently what you are. Your pattern always remains. It is of the subtlest vibratory level. The vibratory level of Spirit is enhanced only by the various layers to create form. Spirit is 100%. Even to say enhanced would at times almost diminish Spirit, almost the opposite of what you see as enhanced.

Spirit sometimes has to struggle so much in form that it diminishes. But, let us say for the purpose of understanding, that Spirit is the purest Light vibration. If it has correlated with the Light well, with the Source as its benefactor, than Spirit retains the very, very subtlest manifestation in the Universe. This means that you can go to the programming called Intent and begin to understand what Spirit is. It comprises all that you are, but when you build upon that in any way, such as I explained in one cell out of ten, thus enhancing by creating a form . . . and I am form. I am not Spirit. Spirit need not be concerned with environment, except vibrational Intent.

"If I could see you, what do you look like?"

I have an august countenance as you might say upon Earth, quite tall, quite how would you say it, perhaps to you supremely severe, but it is not. It is that I have supplanted in my being the countenance of straightforwardness, the ability to perceive things exactly, the way to enact all things as they are notified, instantly, the engagement to perceive the Universe in its totality. This means I don't waste any time. It means I can understand humor as it is applied upon Earth. It is one of the reasons I did thread my way into this device called the form that I am, to understand humor.

If you had lived upon Arcturus since the beginning of time, you would find that humor was one of your lesser assets. Being of an interesting observer character, I chose then to see that other planets have humor and the ability to indulge in humor. Therefore, I chose to become upon Earth.

I know some of the ways humor is held here. I do not understand always why it is humor because I know humor releases an action that is called convulsion in the internal organs. I don't understand yet why humor and the action of convulsion coordinate. I know this is called laughter. I have not yet been able to connect these two, however, I perceive that I am lighter as I am observing the humor and I think that this is connected. There is a lightness to humor which does not endeavor to instruct. Perhaps you can tell me if this is true, or not. There is a way with humor which is intended to alleviate suffering in a certain way and to raise the consciousness vibrations to a certain point releasing through the convulsion called laughter. I believe this is true. Do you see this?"

"I believe the laughter releases tension in the body. I think that is what you will find."

Once when I traveled to the theater with the three of you, I did observe the film through the eyes of this form. I am able to maintain my vibration by integrating as one with this form. I would like to pursue this with your form, but I may not until you have given permission. Spirit may blend more readily and easily and so as not to harm the form of those that they come to, but those of other matter, molecular structure, and denser than etheric . . . spirit, these creatures as we may call ourselves, do not interfere in any way until the appropriate mode is given. So . . . it is an endeavor that we might pursue that I might observe.

"I would very much like you to do that."

Then we will have a notification. We will work out a signal. There will be times appropriate and times not. As you perceive your world, if there are times when my vibration would not enhance the enactment, then that is a time not to do this kind of integration. This form has patterns she uses for those who observe. She can tell you these. Perhaps this will assist.

When I went to the film in the place called theater, I was observing some of the other ones who were laughing, and it seemed that some laughed at one thing and some at another, but indisputedly, those who laughed seemed more able to take the consequence of Earth life vibration. This is very easy to observe being an engineer and being able to see the vibrational attitudes.

I did observe upon entering the theater that certain individuals had an enraptment, or how would you say, an enshroudment of certain vibrations and the laughter released those as to break away bonds. Then, I observed that as they did caricaturize the incidents upon the film that I considered to be at times unnoteworthy, others then thought that they were very humorous.

I appreciate that because I could see that certain things which I had thought to be unnoteworthy were, indeed, quite valuable. Therefore, humor and the convulsion called laughter are tied in with those things not so serious, but very healing, releasing, transcending, and therefore, this is very, very important to the attitudes of forms, especially Arcturians. This is my mission here to observe, assist, and carry back information.

As you would have observed, I can be serious without being heavy. I am not somber, but I am not glib. You can associate with this. I would endeavor to appreciate more humor upon my plane to take back to the colony and to contribute to the endeavor of Arcturian life. It is one thing to be sweet and light, but it can be pious. This is not a very favorable attribute.

"It has been very difficult for me to laugh. I understand that from the Arcturian background. It's . . . it's a very rare person who can make me laugh. I know what you are saying."

If you can perceive that the two of us might do a study of the effects of humor and the actual laughter, we might take this back to the people of Arcturus.

"Michael said that a couple of days ago that one of the main things we are going to have to do is laugh, cheer, to get through the next few years."

Yes, this is going to be, as you say upon Earth, quite tough at times. It is in a mode of your understanding that I reveal to you that, indeed, the time will come when the people will need places of substance to be upon.

I have engineered many feats, one of the least which is the starship design that I came upon. There are other modes that I have designed. These are called cities on your Earth plane, but if you could see Arcturus, they would seem to be enclosed gardens.

Arcturian landscape is not quite what Earth is, therefore, we have created especially valuable dwelling places. To do this within an environment that requires much in the way of stamina and is quite rigorous at times, to have been designed, individual dwellings as well as cityscapes will interest you because you will be taught the ways of manufacturing the domes from the etheric components.

You may not know it was originally not designated that this planet would take all of the growth and turn it into other things. It was thought to be an adornment and a process of environmental enhancement meaning that as you know, the trees are meant for certain things as they grow not as they are harvested. And the seeds and the mountains and the grasses are all intended for certain things. The planet was designed by such an engineer as myself.

"Are there trees and plants on Arcturus?"

There are some. It is to say they are more denoted in the term of the cityscapes being of vast, vast and unlimited possibilities. The cityscapes can cover literally thousands of acres. And even though we use the word city, this is not appropriate because it is very limiting for your minds. It is to incorporate the vast resources that you call forest. Within all of these then live all the people scattered here and there as you might have small communities. So, it is not the same interpretation, and although your understanding is limited, you can know that we move between these communities in . . . in linear fashion much as you would here, in teleportation instantaneously.

"In vehicles that move above the so called ground?"

This is possible, but not so much because teleportation is very, very factual and that is by Intent moving your molecules through the dimensions, but also there are some instances when one would prefer to remain intact and view what you would call landscape.

"Is it a large planet? Are there a lot of Beings?"

It is quite large, but not by the scope of Earth . . . about ¾ to the size. There is less gravitational pull, but not so much as to release the inhabitants to the cosmos.

"Is there water? Are there seas?"

There is fluid much as you would see water. It is an aquamarine in color, but not clear aquamarine—denser color. It is filled with growing material. This you might also compare to some of the fluid upon your planet— that is water with growing things in it. The fluid is located within the cityscapes—city landscapes is a better term.

"And the growing material within the water, is it used for food like our kelp?"

Yes, it is very, very nurturing, and there are components of understanding with the plants of these regions that allows the transference of energy without the ingestion though there is not such a full guttural system as human forms have. This is not necessary.

"Is there a lifespan similar to what there is on Earth, or are people more or less, or Beings—life forms, ageless?"

Not ageless, as you perceive that to be except in terms of Spirit. It is ageless in terms of Earth evaluation being of the mode easily to remain upon Arcturus several thousand years—sometimes to seven or ten thousand. Thus aging is almost unnoticeable. There are some who have characteristics of age. This is because they have been burdened somewhat by their own livelihood.

This is why we speak of humor. This is why we speak of other ways of learning. It is one thing to remain severely adaptable as you might call myself, though light. It is quite another to remain flexible and filled with humor and joy. So, there is an adaptation pattern underway, meaning to circumscribe to some of the other activities in the Universe and add these to the dimension of Arcturus allowing individuals to become more than they have been just as the ones upon Earth are experiencing now.

Do not think that the people of this planet have not any answers at all for the Universe. This is something we must guard against. If any of the people on Earth were to feel that they are second rate Universal citizens, it would destroy all they have done of value upon this planet for the last four billion years. They have tried very hard to find solutions. Let us only say that we would choose to negate those things of violence and circumvent those activities that add to the destruction of the form and the Spirit rather than enhance it.

So, that the people of this planet know they have done what they needed to do and done it well. They have had certain available materials. Some of the materials were thought patterns—vibrational modes.

"Are there certain—can humans in this house, in this apartment, send you certain colors of Light or something that would help you in this 'sleeping room'? What can we do for you?"

Yes, that is my habitation is that what you might call to be pink. It is even of a lighter vibration than this and this along with the white and the gold are my primary usable vibrations. And yes, definitely, this would assist me. Even if you might find such an individual known as the pink quartz, this would help me very much to have a resting stone.

"OK, I will find that for you."

I appreciate this. I do come and go from the Park, but I am more here now because you have come into new awareness. I can be speaking much. This will be a major mode, but not to deny any others to your ways.

"Are there many of you in the park, and do you inhabit that cave by the Lower South Falls?"

It is very sustaining for us being at the foot of the falls and allowing the vibrations of the water to be encased in such a way. Yes, we come and go, although we inhabit the entire park. As you know, teleportation is our way of moving ourselves about. Do not think we cannot be in other places. This is for sustained living—dwelling that I remain here and create a mode to be in. However, we have done this in other places. Even about the fountain in your city hall we have constructed some available environment. Mostly, we are dwelling about the ways of those who are interested in the fundamental beliefs of the Universal Source. Thus, we do not waste a lot of time in the chambers of the government officials.

I would desire that you keep up the way you have started as the BC did suggest with the walking as arranging your molecules into a broader spectrum and then we can be allowed to do some major adjustment for your molecular structure. This will not be to invalidate anything, but rather to enhance the receiving ability of your form.

As I am much concerned about your health in the mode of the food sources, you may perceive it is indeed a category. Let us not be overwhelmed by the fact that many earth foods don't fit. I would suggest that you put away the thought of what you are unable to do and rather enhance what you are able to do thus the healing will appreciate the amount or number of what you may be able to consume.

The Arcturian personality does not have a diffusement of energy. It is very focalized. Perceive that the foods you can eat are a very focalized energy. You do not even know how to measure the quantity of vibrational impact. It is what you are dealing with—that life support system that best enhances your energy, your etheric coding. Now, if you can perceive the more food that comes from pure sources, the more you can eat. Thus packaged items have little value versus fresh.

"I know. I have figured that much out."

Accept in terms of grains. Obviously, grains have to be in a package. Then if you can soak and sprout those grains and allow them to become living . . .

"OK."

the vibrational impact is much different than ground grain or flour, much different and thus the basis of what you can consume will expand. It is known as whole food, but there is more to it than that. It is the vibrational support system for your energy pattern.

"These ones that are here can maybe show me how to do that."

Yes, they know these things inherently, instinctively. It is not to say you may not eat any of the other things the planet offers, but in very small sequence. To be abundantly embracing those things that enhance your energy.

You are not so used to eating food. You came from Orion where food is consumed, but of different substance yet even than here, much, much lighter, even as nectar and fruit. Some grain. Your pattern is not used to food as this having not the gastrointestinal function. The fluid that we speak of, you might indeed compare to what you call spirulina, a rich fluid . . .

"Would that be beneficial for me to get because I have considered that many times?"

Yes, yes, definitely. These ones can implant kelp much more readily. Spirulina would be an enhancement.

"OK."

If you could perceive my form, you would see a tall and very thin character with very similar appendatures as yourselves and with a central core, but not so complex having not to do the functions that your forms do, processing so much food. It is a major function of your form to take the food, process it, and turn it into living cells.

The nature of Arcturus is different from this. The inner form is a solid core of Light so that the extensions are for modes of creativity but not burden, and there is a common comprehension about the form and its abilities upon Arcturus. Many things are accomplished in ways of what you call creature comforts. And the arts, the humanities, and the libraries of our nation are very much like yours, although not accorded into volumes so stressfully, but rather mirrored upon the manner of minds. And, here I ask you to just feel. You can kind of relate it to your microfilms and yet not even stored upon plastic. It is a vibrational mode that is stored and relayed upon sensors. This is very hard to describe.

Channel's husband—"If you can record things, how come you can't just withdraw things from the Akashic records?"

This is that we can. It is to be called in the way of creative that one might begin to think things and then desire to expand as you would of your own accord design something and expand this. Therefore, we record our process much as you would . . .

Channel's husband—"Isn't your process automatically recorded in the Akashic records and then therefore recoverable?"

It is in a mode similar to how you might say that if you created something and someone took a film of you and then put it in a storage facility, yes, you would have access to it. You would have to go to the storage facility. Therefore, as we have form and planetary functions when we have a mode that says we are creating, rather than have that automatically stored in the Akashic records and having then to go to the records and go through those in the etheric . . . you see this is kept differently than you think . . .

Channel's husband—"I just thought the Akashic records would be instant recall. You would just go to the Akashic records and pull out any bit of information that was stored therein immediately without having to do any kind of physical activity. It would almost be like with Intent, you would have the information you wanted out of those records. Evidently, it is not like that."

Do you know how it would be if you decided to design something and you thought about it and it took you several hours and the thoughts came in?

You are going to the records.

"Right."

If I decided I wanted your information, I would have to go to your records. The way we store some of the energy mass for the planet that I live upon is very similar to your library. It is more instant. And, in the library where is stored your creation, I could go to a disc which would spell out in my memory bank exactly what you did instantly, and I could by my Intent go back and forth and reveal to my mind what your mind designed. It is a different method. It is not books, but it is similar to your microfilm. I cannot quite explain to you.

Do you know what a spotlight is like that makes a circle of light upon the ground? This is vibrational matter. And it is a disc. This is similar. Do you see this somewhat?

Channel's husband—"Yes, I see it, and I understand what you are saying. I don't understand the difference between that and the Akashic record."

It is removed. The records are removed and this is instant and it is yours, and it can be tuned back and forth as a dial, back to the first, the middle, the last, back to here. That is different.

"This laughter, this learning that you are trying to do, must be really an important thing or they wouldn't have taken someone of your status on the planet to put them through this."

If it is not light in terms of the mode of the people and the outlook, then the stature of the people begins to be demeaning, and to be abundantly aware of the Universal codes and patterns, we must be inviting some other modes upon the planet. The planet, Arcturus, having been invented upon the beginning of the decades of Light was advanced very rapidly, but then you can get ingrown.

"Yes, and if I can learn what you have come here to teach me, how am I supposed to use what you give me? How am I supposed to teach it?"

That will be made clear as it goes along. That will be made clear.

Channel's husband—"When something becomes funny to us, it is because what is happening is a response to something that isn't a normal response. Do you understand that?"

Yes.

Channel's husband—"So, when you come here and view laughter, how can you get laughter from that when you don't know what our usual response is? You cannot relate to our circumstances or our incidences that create this?"

I take back here you make me feel like it is laughter because I say, "Of course, you are right, this is obvious," and this to me, being a scientist say, this is very funny that this one can know how could I laugh at your incidence, so I think I am learning this is unlikely. Perhaps, this is part of the laughter, the unlikely. Therefore, I take back the statistic that the human beings laugh at the unlikely and that humor then can be founded upon the unlikely. And therefore, what might be to me unlikely might not be to you and vice versa, but as I observe the creature called human and can see what is likely and then I can relate to what is unlikely, and I can indeed experience this thing called laughter.

Now, as I have been in the form that is part of this pattern and I did view this film and I saw what was unlikely because I did not think this film was true enactment. I perceived it was what you would call a sequence of unlikely events. And I now see a word called comedy to describe this. Thus, I could in the time spent, quickly analyze what it was that was considered humorous and I could see that indeed, I agreed this was unlikely and I could begin to feel the laughter in this form. That is a good sequence of training for me to feel the energy of the laughter and the release. It was very healthy, very healing for me. I tend to be in some modes austere, but my austerity is nothing compared to human austerity.

"OK, if that is what you are primarily wanting to learn, then what we will do is try to find situations, because there are many kinds of comedy . . ."

Ahhh . . . yes.

"If you are going to analyze comedy, then there are all sorts of comedy. Lots of times we laugh at our mistakes which is a different kind of comedy. That movie was strictly acting, something as you said, unlikely. That was just someone dressing up and doing something, totally unlike what would be the normal."

I had words from this library—mind—silly, foolish, abundantly inane. I am pulling out words. Capsulizing ingenious behavior—this is another demonstration of what humor might be. The individuals in the film displayed an ingenious behavior. I observed that, indeed, it is quite healthy to be able to laugh as one's own unlikely acts.

"OK, Friday night we are supposed to go to "Crocodile Dundee" and "Startrek 4". "Crocodile Dundee" is supposed to be very funny of a different kind of humor than you saw. We will see if you like that and how different it appears to you or what is different about it."

I shall view these films through your eyes.

"OK."

Therefore, what appeals to you will also allow me to perceive if it also appeals to me in some sort of compatible (that is wrong) comprehensible mode.

"I do not laugh as easily as this other form laughed, and I don't laugh at the silly things as much as she does, so you will see what an Arcturian is like . . ." (Smiles)

You could be trained to alleviate this kind of stringency, could you not?

"I hope so!"

You could loosen the bonds. That is what we are interested in, because the Arcturians have, how would you call it, perhaps a declining health value because of some of the stringencies, and they have been self-imposed since the beginning of time, thinking they are rather important at times. Here you see I may be making a little humor. Arcturians, thinking that they are rather important, have decided that laughter was not a mode they needed to pursue.

"So, you are also telling me that my health will improve if I learn to laugh."

I know instantly of the nature of health and humor. I did read that from the Akashic records and brought it with me. As I observe, I know this to be true. I have not a mode to analyze it within my form, but sitting in another form, yes, I could perceive this, and I believe it, because I perceived the vibrational mode changes. Therefore, I can accurately say that I instantly know this to be true. I need no more data. So, I will tell you, yes.

It is as has been stated that if you are aware of the process of the Source, the Light and the wavelengths, thus the vibrational modes of all things, then you can accrue into a tranquility about how things work, the Wisdoms, the substance all come within their timing. This lets you relax, and thus you can be ready for humor.

That means to be open, aware that something very funny might occur. Then I see you laughing right now. You are relating already to some things that might be unlikely, and even though some things to other people might not be funny, if the laughter is gentle and is not perceived in a way that you call vindictive, then laugher is always appropriate, especially among those that concur to this.

I have not a mode that allows me to perceive ones of Earth who could not concur to laughter. The vitality of the human form is not independent of laughter. It is one and the same.

"I have observed that laughter and music raise my vibrations faster than almost anything else that I can think of."

It is an abundant release of energy from the inner core, and laughter always raises the vibration, never depresses . . . true laughter. It is not corded in any way with those patterns that are depressants. There are many patterns on this planet that are depressive. This is an abundantly releasing energy. (Siren on the street) This is a noise that I hear very much in this city.

"Yes, too much."

It is a siren.

"Yes, always means trouble . . . problems. I really object to being here for that reason."

There is a multitude in this city who have not problems. There is a many ones here who have not a trauma. So, you have a miss that they are here. You must come into the thriving vibrations of those who have joy and let that sound be that of the winged bird, and when it goes by, say, "There he goes again!". This is a way that you can change your thinking.

"OK."

Now, I feel that I must go from this form to allow it to return to balance and I shall be arriving back into the sleeping space approximately three hours from now. I am concurring onto the site of the colony to expand upon this terminology that we have reached.

I shall allow you to be abundantly clear in your Intent in the future about how we may mutually utilize your form. This is significantly what we are speaking of, not to say that I may merge and unmerge at any point in time, but rather that we are making a business arrangement. Here we have a faculty of high perception striding the Earth able to know what is happening. I need not use that faculty at all moments, but some would be quite useful. I can store data.

If you can perceive that the way I would store the data is in a vibrational plane which is paramount to the Light that I spoke about. It is not the vibrational quality of the Source Light, but an actual Light created to store a memory disc. I can do that here and take it back and as I learn, I can create a library of Earth reference discs. 'Tis something that you will understand at another time.

Channel's husband—"We store data in electromagnetic fields, so Light is a vibrational pattern and electromagnetic fields are a vibrational field, so it is kind of the same. It's just a different technology."

Yes. And what I speak of does not take so much equipment. Equipment is getting smaller. I have perceived this. It's very similar. If you think of your computers and discs, you are getting there.

"I am going to the symphony—the Oregon Symphony—tomorrow night. I would invite you to come along and see how you perceive that."

I would like very much to.

"And whatever I can do, you can somehow let me know and if there is something you need . . . I will get the rose quartz. If there is something else, we will do it."

This is sufficient. Just your time, this is a point we will make at a future date. We will begin to be subsisting more together in this training time, learning time from both sides. I am learning and at the same time, you are being trained, so we are exchanging energy. And here then, it is your pattern that will enhance your work. This is how the training will be utilized upon earth. You will just know more. You will be completely hooked into your systems. This is not time to even think about it yet. It is coming soon.

Now, I grant thee good grace and have a safe way, and you also, and it is very much desired that I accompany you to the symphony. It would be quite grand. You may find you have quite an entourage at the symphony!

"Thank you. Thank you for being in my house."

Oh, you are very welcome, and I thank you for the space, and be well here.

Chapter 2

Holanea, Commander of the Arcturian Fleet on Earth

A few months went by, Gayl made another trip to this area and we went for the day to the coast. It was a cloudy, windy day, the waves were crashing in and we were in a picnic area at a beach south of Lincoln City, Oregon. Gayl let me know that ones wanted to talk to me, so we sat down on a picnic table and my training continued.

I am called Holanea and I am channeling to you from the planet called Arcturus. To implement best to you, I choose to manifest in this manner although there are other modes that I may come to you. The mode of my actualization is this actual realm that you exist in. The mode of my actualization is within a perspective that you can perceive which you can come into. This mode is a spatial dimension that you must accrue to. You will receive instructions.

This is your mode also from a prior time. This is not an experiment. This is an actualization. It is important that you differentiate for there are those on your planet who will be experimenting. This is not necessary. It is particularly not necessary in this moment in time for you—moment being your form upon Earth, only a moment in actuality.

This moment that you experience is a mode that you applied to, for, and became. It is your purpose, your mission. From the mode that is called Arcturus, there is another mode manifesting that is your mission. Your mission upon Earth being to pervade the Light in matter attestable to by other forms. Do you perceive what I say?

"Yes."

It must be not only an action and in perception through instruction but it must be by atmospheric vibration carrying the engenderment of your planet. This is perfection . . .

"of the planet Arcturus."

You carry the engenderment of the planet. It has two manifestations, one which can be rather irritating is that you always want things to be just right, but another, which is not irritating is that you manifest the highest degree of compatibility of actual limitation of the Light. This is not something Earth people are used to. The compatibility is actually implanting of the Light energy, the beams . . . the beams of the totality within your physical system within your mode of living. This is the perfection of all things. Do you see this?

"Yes."

The precision with which you approach the things you do comes from this. The actualization comes from this. The hesitation that you spoke of once before is not to negate, it is earth mode interference.

I come to you now to say there will be training that will bypass this Earth mode interference. There will be training that you will perceive of your own accord. You will not need such a connection facilitator. You have been instructed where to be for the beginning connections. It is a place you have been to yesterday at this time.

As you perceive, the connection will not be even in the etheric. There will be much more to the connection than I can tell you at this time. There will be instruction in many ways. It will pertain to the connection. It will pertain to your availability to the instruction. There will be times when you will not be able to receive well because of earth mode interference, but as we proceed, that will be less. You will rise above it and go beyond.

It is not inconvenient that you exist now in Earth mode. It is pertinent. Do not negate any of the Earth mode. It is important. As you perceive your instruction, as you understand more what you are, you will bypass . . . you will look beyond, know beyond and you will integrate with Earth mode. This is where you have been trained. The difference you perceive what was and what is in your Earth mode . . . your level has happened. It has concluded a time.

This is the beginning of a vast, vast region of knowing. It is interspatial. It is different. It opens into the dimensions of your past endeavors of those who support your work here. The actual of your work will come to you. Your criteria for your work represents your Beingness. Knowing of your Beingness, your totality releases the work. Do not deviate from what you have begun. Do not be concerned. It will change of its own accord. It will come through various instruction. You will be made aware of your connection. It will be absolute. You will have no doubt. There will be manner of conference, in your terms, conversation. It will not be in a lecture format. You are not a student.

You are a foremost Master. I speak now in this tone because I want you to know I am real, that I exist, that I am not in a parlay fashioned . . . I am here, strong, clear and as a co-worker. For awhile, I will be a teacher. That will change. We will co-exist in manner of teachers. You are not to consider yourself subjected in any manner. You are totally the representative in this region for the work of the One. You are from a highly evolved civilization.

You do not need to fear whether the ones of Earth will accept what you bring. It is not important. You are to concentrate on the actualization of the work. Do not expect anything of these ones who come to you. Do not even expect that they would appear each time. Do let them have completely their own will thinking that it is a release that is mandatory.

You have beyond their own dignity, your form to consider. Do not bind yourself to any. You come from the One, you are to return to the One. That is all there is. The form . . . that is all there is to consider. As you serve yourself and therefore all, none have any complimentary action to yours except as they serve. You are complete. All those who serve will know it and link and the energies will grow together by accord.

The ones who go upwards against the current will be diffused. They will not be of your stream of consciousness. It will not be necessary to carry them with you, nor to do anything except observe them. Those who are with you will go each on their own accord, each responsible as individuals of Light varied. Therefore, there are no dependencies.

You will bring other cognizance into the atmosphere of your teaching but they will be of the same current. This will happen many times. Ones will come about you, you will touch, bond and go on. You will not have loneliness. There will be many building around you, but it is very important to remember that you need not depend on each other. You just are. It is what you have been taught.

As you have the feeling of being alone, that is purposeful to put you in a realm where I am and I will come at appropriate times to begin the interactions. It is to bring you into a dimension of understanding that form exists for convenience and purpose. It is not habitual. It is not necessary unless it suits. You are not forced into form. I do not have form now. I am a full fledged citizen of Arcturus and the Universe. I need not be encased at this time. Other times I have chosen. Upon your planet, there are forms and not forms that exist side by side. It is different up here.

Your form moves passing beyond form. This has to happen to you alone. It could not happen with another. You, yourself will know when you are ready to step into my realm. I will not come to yours except in this way, but I will be there as completely as you and others of your category also . . . your aides so to speak. This is not the Legions that she speaks of. This is different. Your personal, (entourage is not the name,) your personal cabinet will be about you. They will qualify themselves to you. They will speak of themselves and how they are. They will have names. They will have personalities. They will have administrative duties, but ours is administration where yours is enactment and the Legions support the whole thing.

We have no frivolous moments at this time. We have humor, but on Arcturus we tend to be light in word and deed and the ways of others balance that. There is a reason for going to Arcturus. It is your Mother Planet. You were drawn there. You have been many places. After this we suggest you go to Venus for awhile to be a citizen in Light and light heartedness and complete abandonment. You are from Arcturus.

I am not comfortable with other ways, but I do go to those ways because I am learning. I do not abandon a more stilted atmosphere of the planet and I find it to be comforting as well as convenient as well as efficient.

Now, as I speak to you here, there is a demeanor coming that will envelop you. It will become your way. It will seem to soften the edges, but what it really will do is bind them. It is the glue that you seek and you will become more mellow because of your confidence. It will not be abrupt. It will be as a seaming together and it will be set. Your soul being and ones will know it as they come about. It will be your relaxation. You will meet others from Arcturus who are informed after a time, after a time. You will recognize them. It will not matter that they are there. It will just be, "Hello there. Good to see you here."

So, it concludes this discussion. We will begin again next week. We will wait until the time is appropriate and be thinking of these events we have discussed. There is an implementation I desire that is that you do not, please, disperse energy into more learnings of other nature right at this time. More leave the spaces where you might read or listen available for this, for the interpretation of your way, your own mode.

Your instruction will be direct. It will not be through another source. Therefore, you must leave the times available. This comes in contemplation. This comes in comfort zones where nothing else is interfering. Sometimes this takes several hours to achieve. Music is a very good way to achieve, but be aware not to accompany the music with reading. Leave great quantities of time for this, otherwise you cannot not accomplish it. Later it will not matter. It will be done.

I go now. I bid you good night.

"Thank you for coming."

You are very welcome.

"Holanea is Commander of the Arcturian delegation on earth. That was like a message from home. I can understand that sternness."

Channel—"Wow!! That was powerful energy!!

Chapter 3

Rozann's 1st Visit and Aleckatron's 2nd Visit

I am one called Rosie to you.

"Hello, Rosie."

I have an abundance of energy that has allowed her to feel my entry. As I would have come sooner, she would have known sooner, also. I did not negate any of the conversing. It is only that I must enter upon a certain arrival time. It is not to denote that there must be change. Do not allow ones to come about and dictate their ways to you. It is always upon observance of custom.

"I don't understand what you are saying. I don't understand what you mean."

If I come to perceive that you be in conversation, it is only that I must enter in order to exist . . .

"I see."

so that I do not say to stop conversing, I only say that I must enter. Now, I know that at another time, there are some that are so familiar, they may say, "It is I and I must talk." That is their way and that is fine. I have no occurrence to do this in my custom. I have only to be about in a pattern of courtesy, congeniality. That I do not understand the customs of others is no happenstance, I have been out of the way for a long time. I ask that I might observe these times through your form when you think it is appropriate.

"You may, Rosie, that's fine."

I do not know that I have the vibratory implantation that can be considered comfortable. Therefore, we can be making the adjustments. You can say, "It is not quite right." If I have too much warmth, it is that I have not sufficiently deterred the energy.

As you perceive that I have come from your home to a way here, it is not to completely annihilate the old ways, but yet to become one with the environment and the pattern of the people that we adjure to. As I would become one, it is not to become different than I am but to make certain acquiescence unto the way so that I am not interfering. As I would say, I have customs of your way to teach you, and you can, at the same time teach me about ways that are of Earth.

"OK."

I have not known these ways at any time before now, ever. I have come accustomed to a vibratory rate that is far finer than I am now. Perhaps even the rate that I am in is too condensed and perhaps I can raise it and that will make the less heat. The higher the rate, the lighter the substance and therefore, the less noticeable the implant.

"You have a great deal of energy that I can feel."

Ummhmmm. I can abide by less energy here. Perhaps I can accrue to that at this time. I am trying to rise above slightly to lessen the rate.

"It's not uncomfortable for me, Rosie, unless she is."

No, she is well. This is well for me. I can see how the (yes, this is well the adjustment is made) as I become more familiar, I can again adjust. The one called Aleckatron is very efficient at these matters. I shall ask that it be a motive that he teach me.

I do not have abundant energy to stay long. I have been able to stay within the confines of the sleeping room to a degree and then upon the colony base which is upon the falls. I then must be coming from a different source of energy to here and back. I shall be able to accustom myself as time goes along.

As you would occur to the one named Aleckatron, there is a mode you can establish within the sleeping room, it is to become with the etheric pattern there to the combustion of your energy and Intent, creating daily a pattern that is called mostly rose quartz. This will give you an idea of the molecular structure in the etheric. As you would perceive that you would implant into the room, perhaps, a very, very large etheric rose quartz stone. It could be a method that would enable the atmosphere to be sustaining not only to yourself because you have come from this way that is similar in molecular structure. It would also assist the ones who come about you, and as the mode is struck somewhat already with your notice of the small stone, you can implant that same theory into the entire room. That you would walk into a room . . . you can also walk into a stone.

"OK."

I feel that my rate is making her nuances difficult. Therefore, I will withdraw as I know this is being something of an irritation. I will work with this. It is not quite coordinated. I do desire that as I come to you, you not allow anything that is beyond your mode. This is a promise from you else I cannot enter into your form. If it is not appropriate, you must speak so.

"OK".

And then I can learn because I can withdraw and begin again. And that is what we do.

"OK".

The rose quartz is not an implantation that would harm you. It is well for your Arcturian energy. Now, I suffer not, nor does this form. We are compatible and it is appropriate that at this time, I do remove myself.

"Thank you."

You are welcome.

Channel—My throat was vibrating really fast almost like I couldn't talk. That was neat. He needs to practice. The vibratory rate was a different . . . it wasn't the form vibratory rate which was what Aleckatron told us. It was a different molecular structure and I think I had a lot more of his structure, but then at a lower rate than Aleckatron, so you feel that heat, especially, almost raspy. It will be easy for them to make that adjustment. Ok, let's just see who comes . . . .

Aleckatron's Second Visit

I am indeed called the one, Aleckatron.

"Hello."

As I would have this mode upon this way, the one called Rozann is of a different mode slightly because he is recently arrived. He is well onto the way of his work. It will not be hard, for now I have a vibratory rate that is instantly more similar, but as you can tell, it is different from some others. The way that you can determine the finest of the rate as you listen to such a discourse is by the volume and quality of the voice. This does not mean good or bad, it is only that there are different inflections that give you clues, and thus at a time in the future, you will be able to determine the source energy even without the name.

As human beings have inflections upon their voice, so others have their rates.

"Tell me more about the rose quartz stone for the etheric. That's not to be the entire room, but just a portion of the room?"

If you like, the entire room can be of this mode. It is effective for you, also. It is not a mode that is discouraged for you at all, but rather to see that the entire room can be implanted with the etheric stone and this being of a particular structure that will allow you to be nurtured in your home base vibrations, and this would be very good for you.

"OK."

It is not something that you have to do.

"Is this something that is one-sided? Is this something that I put there in the etheric and not something that we do together?"

We can help to maintain it. We have already begun this. But such a large project is endeavored so much alone, also it is not occurring without your consent. As you perceive that you at once may do this, if you choose to reverse, also you can. To say etheric is somewhat a misnomer, it is that once you decide to create such an absolute, you are bringing together the qualities of that molecular structure.

"The dream that I had a few nights ago about the big crystal in the middle of a circle, was that something that you are doing with me? Was that something that you are teaching me? Is there a reason for that?"

Coming into your time, there will be far more work with the crystals and the way of the work will be taught to you. You do not have to know.

"So you would rather I not took the lessons from Linda?"

Linda is not of Arcturian energy, and therefore, she will not give you the specific instructions that can be given you by your own coding, but what she teaches is of benefit, and so far as it is known to be more among the people, the better.

"OK."

In addition, you can learn from your Source energy and share with her.

Absolutely.

"I feel, and I don't mean it in an arrogant way, that perhaps I can soften her use of crystals. Her way is pretty harsh."

Yes, she is coming to learn again. This is important for one of her demeanor and her empowerment. She is not to be mean to the crystal. She is not knowing of their absolute truth.

"Yes."

As she has come from Venus, then she can be escaping into that mode also, which is the lighter approach, and as you are incorporating mutual energy, you will exchange much, and the way that she has been can become more softened and clear and then your knowing heightened, also.

"All right."

It can be a mode that is then incorporating more energy than each of you has at this time.

"I'm a bit cautious because it's not a time in my learning when I want to go backwards. I don't want to get the wrong learning and then have to take years to . . . ."

This is not wrong. This is to say that it will not be an absolute as you are expanding into a new concept with the one called Linda. Call it a basic support system for much, much more. Tell her of this and that there will be many more things coming to you that can be laid upon the base system that she gives you.

"OK."

Defer to her that there will be more for her, also, to use.

"OK."

The basic methods of the use of stones is not so clearly understood among many. There are some very, very specific methods and these cannot be granted upon the general public very easily. Some of the methods that are being taught are squandering energy. For one thing to blatantly invoke the crystals beyond their means or without their consent and without the advise of their personal systems is not an efficient use of energy, nor courteous.

As I would see that you have been known to many in your land by the crystals themselves, as you have been a healer with the crystals themselves, then you are here expected to continue that, and that advice and that connection will be made very, very clearly once you have stemmed the tide of energy that is not sufficient to your needs called taxes. Then more things can come.

As you now know, you may be in a way that is much more advanced than you can comprehend. I tell you these things so you can come into a new acknowledgement as your substance in form. Your form enactment is far beyond your expectations even. Your considerable energy is nothing as comprehended with what can be given. It is not Earth energy and it does not have to be deployed in Earth pursuits, but can be merely channeled as existing energy and that means through the clarity of your existence here, it can become one with the people you come to. It is not even something you have to tell.

I tell you this because the blasts of energy that will be coming to the Earth surface will be far beyond what you can even comprehend now. I want you to be aware of the prolonged existence of your ability and your acquirement of disciplines that occurred before you came to this planet. I do not want you negating one thing. Do not comprehend that you explain how you came to be the teacher that you are.

Tell that you are teacher. This is the way of the speakers of Arcturus to say with pride, "I came as Teacher." There is nothing more to say except that as you choose to help others understand, not to qualify. It will be evident, and what you perceive of yourself is so little understood even by yourself that you can almost set it aside. You have become now I tell you as the empty vessel waiting for your Soul Self to enter.

It is not Arcturian energy that surrounds you at this time. Do not let another tell you what you are, but let them experience the entrance of you as soul emersed. That is coming very, very soon within a few days. The complete emersion of Soul is begun. Had you not agreed, we would not have proceeded.

"So that is part of the reason you are here, to help that come together?"

Yes, yes. As Soul Self of you begins its merger, then there can be no other comprehension but that, and you will know. Now as the sequence is begun, there is no Arcturian energy except those that are of your mode. The Arcturian energy is coming to you. Do you see this?

"Yes."

You are devoid of other principles. We remove all of the life source energy you have stored so long upon this planet. Do not be dismayed that perhaps it was useless. It was very absolute training. What I want is that you are of a mode, that is the way of Arcturus. It is the highest form of Light. There is none higher.

"I understand that."

There is no kind of acquiescence and yet there is no kind of resistance from other ways. Other ways are all let to their own Beingness. The complete and pure form of Light is absolute love with no question about what one is or another is.

Now, as I tell you that there is none other than Arcturian energy in your Beingness, it is only that you are swept clean, ready. Everything that you have learned here is to implement this entry, so you do not have to be attached to what you have learned, but letting it flow through as a free and abundant material resource. Do you see the difference?

"I think so. What you are telling me is what I need to depend on for learning is what comes in . . ."

Yes.

"And that the books and seminars etc. that I have attended are simply resource material."

Yes. Yes. And they are not to be accounted to.

"If the information that I get is different, I am to rely on what I get."

Yes. It can be merged, however, and it can be added in a way that is soft.

"I understand both of those ways."

I want you to understand so clearly that your training has been to equip you for the work you are doing, but now that it is only training. It is not self.

"I understand that, too."

And it is also that you can rely upon all that you are—to become pure Light and not have havoc. My dear sister, it is not time for you to have havoc of any kind. Do not let another's ways become as an instrument of penalty as when you go to the form called office and they say things, do not let any way of distress come about you. Understand it is being taken care of. Ask. As ones speak out of turn, do state to them, but do not let it weigh upon you like a stone. Let it float away like a feather. The Arcturian Legions are around you, beside you, in front and behind. Never are you alone. I cannot tell you of the love you are given.

"Are there fewer of us? Are we less percentage wise on Earth than some of the others? Are there less Arcturians?"

Yes . . . yes . . . yes. This is not a domination factor by any, but yet the Arcturians have not so abundant a population as to squander all upon the surface. Some are left behind to do the tending of the planet, and yet some must come who are so powerful as to be able to make the changes that are necessary.

"What our basis is here is to keep them(Earth Beings) out of the rut?"

Yes.

"Even the ones who are Lightworkers study and study but they study the same things . . . they don't seem to see that they need to move on."

Yes. They sometimes cannot see the broad and yet sometimes they see too broadly and it is the balance in the seeking as well as in all things, but I here return to what I choose most for you to know, that in the seriousness of the Arcturian countenance, there is still the understanding of pure love. I want you to really be aware that you are this pure Light and that nothing can burden you. It truly cannot, but it is a choice factor now in your life to let it float away and not take upon any other's ways in any mode.

As for the abundance of energy available to you, it cannot be given so freely as to when you completely clear away everything else. We are moving the vibrations away from you that have abundantly burdened you. We are doing it. As you by your thought, then, assist, we can come with more for you that is your right. And as others come into their knowing, allow them the benefit of your high vibrations by your presence.

"I still have, not as much as before, but I still have doubts. This will be a test for me if I go ahead with these people because some of them seem to be very knowledgeable. My knowledge is more general and I feel that I don't know as much as they do. I know that I know more on the whole than they do. I have no doubt about that. I have been persecuted too many times in my lives. It's a pattern and it's hard to break."

(Aleckatron is talking to me about changing real estate offices and my knowing a lot about residential real estate, but very little about the area and how things are done here. At the time this was given, I was teaching a series of spirituality classes that I had written to groups of people and was getting hate mail at the real estate office because of my use of crystals and the teaching of that material.

For several years, as I got more involved in selling real estate to make a living and more involved with the people I was working with, I became very stressed. In order to be able to bring in all of the connections that the Arcturians were setting me up to do, I would have needed much more quiet, free time than I had.

For this reason, as I became busier and busier, I was never able to connect with their energy on my own, without the help of my channel friend, Gayl. However, I was well aware that I was knowing more. I could tell when they were working with me and that my accumulation of knowledge was much greater and many times I knew when they were looking through my eyes.)

Aleckatron continues—But you perceive that you have come from a way that could be called Commander of the Legions. Now, should the Commander run each ship or should the Commander set a standard for others to see upon and appeal to and understand and be comforted by? It matters not that you do not know the nuances of every single thing. The fact that you care enough to collect the information, give it back out in abundance and more as it comes and then tell straight to the ones.

I have not every detail, but I care not for that. My job is to help you reach out further and in the reaching, we shall both learn. Be not embarrassed or afraid to say such words. Do not take heavy burden for that which you are doing or not doing. Allow it to float lightly to the sequences and invite the others to add to that. In appropriate time, not to inundate you, you might each class leave a time to share that they can do this.

"I will do that."

The wise teacher always knows that they do not know all. It is abundantly clear that no one knows all, even God, and that is why we are all Being. You can say this. I now give you in accord that you are mine own and that we have come together here, and for now it is not good that I stay for my energy is dwindling as you can perceive. I have not the abundance that I have had. I have been too much about. We all must go back into the forest and stay there a time. Do not expect us just now for several days, but do not be a-feared for we have not long to get here.

"OK."

If you choose to be with us merely call and be not a-feared that we will not come. We have just been too busy and I fear too nosy.

You have an apparatus called a discible (in the etheric on my head) and it is kind of an extension point—almost like you have a helmet with a point. It is a very brilliant shaft of light, and you can call in this energy at will, but it is abundantly clear that you must let go of the other things to hear this. Do not be frustrated and rushed about how this comes. It will come. It is coming. You have now been taking messages and you know it. Don't dissuade that. Just let it be. Don't rush it. Just let it be. Don't be a-feared it will stop. Just let it be. It will become stronger and stronger.

Now I go.

"Have a good rest and say 'Hello' to the others."

I shall. There are about thirty.

"I was going to ask you how many."

Yes, they shall come from time to time here.

"We will work on the rock. I tried to find you another stone. I will keep trying. It's too far away from the Montana mountains. I could get it easily there."

But, the etheric will suffice and I thank you so much. Good night.

Channel—"Those guys . . . those guys are big time stuff!!"

Comments from Joyce—Gayl says the discible which sits etherically on my head (this is what the word sounds like—may not be the correct spelling) looks like a dunce cap! I was told that I should never have my ears pierced because it would interfere with the energy coming through this apparatus. For that reason, I have never had my ears pierced.

You will note as you read this material the intelligence of these Beings, their vocabulary, their concern for me. Never in the years I worked with them did they want to overburden me with anything or want me to be uncomfortable. They only wanted to help me.

Yes, they were studying me because they understood my Arcturian background and as one of the later ones said, "You live here and you are Arcturian, so I thought I could, too." They would never work with me in any way without my permission. I found them all to be of the same intelligent, wise, loving, gentle energy.

Because of this, it pains me a lot when I hear through the media that ALL space Beings's are coming here to annihilate us. That couldn't be further from the Truth.

Ashtar, Commander of the Galactic Command that oversees this sector of the Milky Way Galaxy, made his first appearance on Earth in 1952 when we were attempting to detonate the hydrogen bomb. Nothing of a nuclear nature will be tolerated by the Galactic Federation because already there have been too many previous disasters using nuclear energy. The continents of Atlantis and Lemuria were destroyed in a thermonuclear war that left only the continent of Australia and smaller islands remaining. The deserts of Sahara, Gobi, some in the Western United States, and the Australian Outback are all remains of this thermonuclear war. The rings of Saturn are remnants of the planet, Maldek, which was blown up by nuclear energy.

Planet Earth has not been part of the Galactic Federation for eons of time because of its violence.

Inside our Earth planet, almost 6 million people, who are the highly evolved remainder of the continents of Lemuria and Atlantis have lived and evolved for thousands of years. This information, also, has been hidden from us by our Illuminati controlled governments, but excellent information can be found on Telos, which is one of five cities inside Mt. Shasta containing 1.5 million people, in books channeled by both Dianne Robbins and Aurelia Louise Jones, as well as life in "The Hollow Earth" channeled by Dianne Robbins and in the monumental work called "The Seven Sacred Flames" channeled by Aurelia Louise Jones. You might also check out "Admiral Byrd's Flight Into the Hollow Earth" which has finally been released after having a gag order for 64 years!

Should the underground nuclear tests and our use of nuclear energy been allowed to escalate, think of how many souls both on and inside the planet would have been destroyed. Considering the probability that all of those Beings also have parallel lives and lives on other planets and stars going on at the same time, the horrendous damage would have been incalculable.

Those inside the planet had already come to the realization that war, of any kind, stifled growth, so they chose to live in caves that they have made into fabulous cities over the past thousands of years where they could evolve in peace and harmony. They will be making their reentry to the surface as soon as our vibrations here on the surface are high enough that it is safe for them to emerge.

Without those from outer space, this planet would have turned on its axis in the 1990's. There were photographs of ships taken above Russia where the ships were sending beams of green Light to hold the planet in place. The starships that patrol our skies, are in contact with the cetaceans, the whales and dolphins, who monitor the pollution in our oceans. The ships also monitor the decline of our ecosystem.

Why do you suppose the huge oil spill in the Gulf of Mexico seemed to be under control before it did as much damage as it could have done in our aquafirs? The enzymes that helped speed the process were a gift from our space brothers and sisters who also "do everything possible without violation of our free will to neutralize excess radiation within our soil and atmosphere and to deflect potentially dangerous asteroids from impacting our planet." (Taken from "The Ashtar Galactic Command" by Ashtar-Athena SherAn from the book "Message from the Hollow Earth", pgs 194 and 195.)

Relieving pressure on the tectonic plates so that the earthquakes Mother Gaia needs to release pressure on her surface is another of the jobs taken on by the star fleets. With their help and technical assistance, it is possible to turn a potentially harmful quake into several smaller ones that do not create the huge life threatening tsunamis. And, as soon as our consciousness rises to a point where they can land safely, the starships will bring countless new technologies, including free energy to this planet.

The Ashtar Command is composed of thousands of starships and millions of personnel from many civilizations. Some of us live here on Earth, and others originate far out of this star system, but we all work toward bringing this beautiful planet into peace and harmony and the 5th Dimension.

Yes, there have been many "bad guys" from space, just as there have been on the surface, but let's know that the ones from the Ashtar Command and the Galactic Federation are universal ambassadors of peace, peacemaker/ diplomats and peacekeepers—and I tell you that from first hand experience!

Chapter 4

Kortron

May 7, 1988

Are you present?

"We are."

Good. I am Kortron. I am from a planetary system called Seldon (?). It is a dimension not known to you freely, but you shall come to know this. Yes, they are here, too. (Meaning the Arcturians.)

"Yes, they are." (I always know when they are present because my nose gets very itchy!)

When you have these occasions known as this space . . . may I speak to you upon terms of authority. I have commanded a large Confederation. I am part of a Legion that incorporates about three billion processes meaning to you that I have ships under my command, I have personnel under my command, I have systems under my command, each being a unit of energy. As planets come into their substantial raised level, these also are put under my command. All of this I confer to you as you are the auspices of that which speaks for Sananda. Do you understand what I have just said?

I am of yours. I am your servant. My command is at your disposal. When we come into this kind of interaction, we become as we have been before. Do not think for a moment that we waste a moment. We become in these interactions as we have been before in full service. Perhaps you wonder why each one speaking is from off planet. It is because you were called together. It is a council meeting of the highest order that you are exhibiting. When you become into this essence of your being, you state to us that you are available and ready to hear.

It is not an order that you appear. You are drawn by your resonance. When you are ready you make that access. It is known. It is through your tone. Some of you are new to this, you think. Some of you are old to this, you think. It is all the same. It has nothing to do with Earth knowledge. It has to do with opening. It has to do with availability. It has to do with awareness. The level of understanding that is exhibited has less to do with it than your vibrational frequency, when you understand that is Earth's. When you are at the frequency that you can hear, then you will understand whatever you hear. Do you understand this?

"Yes."

(Chuckles) Now, when the Confederation put into auspices (meaning sponsorship), its people upon the planet Earth, upon the joint venture that is called Mission Earth Healing, to put it in very short terms, let us say that there are so many that you cannot count them, but past trillions, past trillions of billions of individuals and working units. Thus I appear to you to state, "It is important. It is time." Ashtar comes often because he has the ability to raise your vibrations to accept this kind of integrity.

If you could see me, it would be much as the one you have drawn. I am very, very tall, nine feet easily and very thin in your thinking and extremely powerful. I have ship commander status, but that is nothing compared to the role that I must assume now. I expect things, and this you may find a surprise because you are being told not to have expectations. It is different to expect things. It is different to expect performance from those who have agreed. Do you understand this?

"Yes."

When you sign your mandate, when you agree by blueprint to come forth, when you design and incorporate that into your living structure, the pattern that you will follow upon Earth, when you design this before you inhabited flesh, it was in much confidence, in much interaction, in much seclusion with various members of various fleets to determine the best approach for you and the best way that you could exhibit it and the way that you could stay healthy. In other words, you did not come into flesh to exhibit recreational purposes. Although you are free to do that here, that is your choice and you must to maintain yourself. This is not a playground.

When you can hear the words that have been stated to you before this time, I must say that you are ready to hear of the Highest Commands. When you chose to come to Earth, each of you mandated, and you know this already, it is a purposeful message to state, the mandates are being fulfilled. When you come present, it is time to be stronger with knowledge because that exhibits you with your strength and gives you availability to higher sensitivities. If you always want to play the game of lower intelligence and lessened sensitivities, you will be left at that post. Understand this, it is not my choice, it is yours, and all the others. Step forth and state, "I am strong and I am ready", and you will receive greater instructions. It is a liberating factor because the strength of your being allows you to become more, or you can hide that. It is your choice. Again, I demonstrate no remorse upon one's choice, but when one steps forward, I then expect them to remain at post. I do not expect the dance to and back. Then I cannot count the numbers. The resonance is not secure.

If you look upon the grid that you have asked about before this time, you will see that the electronic signals which are sent from the ships are miles and miles and miles apart, and yet circumvent the distance. And this tapestry as it is woven is sometimes interchanged and meets molecular needs. That is why it is a tapestry and not a grid.

But it is emanated at certain signal points and those ships are spaced about the planet, at precise positions . . . this allows each surface millimeter to be nurtured . . . each surface millimeter to be nurtured. Without this, you could not survive. Human beings could not survive.

OK, when we have this ability coming from celestial starships, the governing factor upon Earth that is necessary becomes less. That means you need not become enamored of the ritual of planning and patterning, but this means that you need to be very, very aware of your post. It needs your attention, not to become a compulsion, not to become a fanaticist, to become a way of life of merger between physical and etheric duellas, so that I as a post commander, not in charge of you, but one of you, I can come to your midst and state, "This is what is happening. Be aware that this is coming. Be aware that we notice changes and we have devised a way to meet that need. Be aware that this is our attempt. Be aware that you are part of a merger energy that will allow others to move into their positions."

Do you surmise how you might apprise the resonance of the total, and when you leave each of you become individuals again, but a resonance as a total that allows certain things to take place in the upper atmosphere. When you gather, it becomes a spiral energy. When you are positioned then, it becomes into an actual databank. You are not machines, you are not tools, you are instruments of Light.

(Much louder) When I speak to you strongly in these terms, it is because I am positioned to do this. It is also my trait. Hmmp. Hmmp. I have the ability. I do not mind. I also have compassion, otherwise, I would not be standing here.

If any of you think for one minute that we would ask that the planet be devastated, erase this. We have the desire to allow the healing energies to be established and nurtured and focused. It is veritably possible to heal an entire planet while you are meditating by being with that as an exposition, but we are past that time. If we had begun that action when the one called Jesus, my friends, strided across your planet, we could have done that. We are past that time. We have no more time to do this, but you will be glad to know we can suffice. We can bring into play in other manifestations.

When we as ship commanders designate the rays that will allow a vibrational tone to meet and merge and weave itself about the planet, it superimposes over the decay an ability to rise. It superimposes over the density, the distress, the violence, the war games, the ability to reach out for peace. It superimposes the thought that states, "If we cooperate with the Goddess, we are head of the chemical impositions. In the midst of this that is decay and imposition, someone is saying "Wait, wait, we can do it this way," and they are on their hands and knees. Now that is coming from higher energy sources that are available.

When you came, you brought those sources. You brought them with you. Your support system is superimposed. It is not just for you, however, and those of your kind, it is for others who dwell upon this planet who are permanently called the masses. When masses become entrenched upon this planet, they tend to go into form and out of form and into form and out of form and they tend to do this very fast dance without circumventing that which is the loss. They tend to carry the loss with them and come back and expand upon it. It is a burden upon both sides of the veil. It is very difficult for those who are in charge of that realm just beyond life form. It is unmanageable. There are throngs trying to figure out what to do. The imposition of energy allows them also to become Light and to move unto the Light patterns and decide what they want to do instead of being sucked back into the disturbance.

If I say to you that I am a Commander, that is a side job compared to the rest of the work I do. It is not important to delineate that further, but I also may say that you, also, are capable of many more things than you imagine, many things, and they can fit perfectly into the sustenance of your Being. Your Self can allow this to be. Your Self can absorb from the Cosmos that which you have been, that which you will be.

Did you know that you can pull forth to you that which is called future and utilize that future? When you state that I am ready. I need to know more. How rewarding it is, how grand it is to stand before you and state who I am and what you are so that you can grow further from that moment, if you allow yourselves to see. You are not so much different than I. Physically, yes, perhaps. Perhaps not. Perhaps the real you is nine feet tall, very tall and perhaps you also have grown upon wings that are not from angels, but body.

So, as we expect each other to behave in that capacity, we have assurance it is all right to expect that from your fellows. It is all right to be able to be secure in the demonstration of confidence. Don't confuse that with expectation. We have two entirely different values. When the weaving is applied, it allows you to draw from the resonance that is most important.

Available to you and by your position, there is that which you need. If you moved yourself willfully to another position, you would be in a resonance that is not yours. You may think it is Earth. It is not. There are Light bearers there and they have the resonance they need. It is matched. That is why it is so important to hear, to ask what is best now, or to just wait and know that it is well. And to know that no matter what the guidance is, it is considering your total need.

I will tell you very surely, and I swear to you this that there will be times you will be asked to do things you would rather not, moves you would rather not, places you would rather not speak out, people you would rather not speak to, but I swear to you, we must. I must do things I would rather not in a different time. You are like me. You are as strong. You will be asked to move forth and then draw back. Do not be afraid at those moments. You are not being put up for ridicule. You are being put into position.

It is not important to honor the old ways of Earth past consideration. Earth is in the dynamics of change. She has become alive. She is ordering her cause. She will speak. We support that. You are we. We then supply your needs more than you can even guess. We then become one with you. We then bestow the energy of the spheres upon you. We then become in our way complete because you know us.

If you do not know us, if you do not step to post, if you do not accept the dynamics of this mission, it is much more than asking for tranquility among the people, it is much more . . . it is action. When you come forward, it frees us. If you deny us, we are not complete, but also neither are you, and all those who would come into these positions come to know this. You come to strength, fullness. And it is private until the moment when you know you must share and you will know just how much. If that person standing before you can only hear this much, maybe the words, "God Is, and you are a part of God". That may be all they can hear. I assure you that is enough. They need no more.

There may be a person you have never seen before and you must tell them about this conversation, and you know and they know it, and they hear it and they open fast and fast and fast. And they stepped close in that moment and you know it. You give them references to others. You can continue that with them. And the way that this will work is that we each know one another so well that we can discuss possibilities of action, so well that we can disagree, so well that we can be chagrined with one another and state, "Leave me alone now. I know how this might be."

Be so familiar with your power that you are yourself. It is now that you can take this unto your own ways. No other can dictate to you. And in those same terms we have mandated. We have designed for ourselves a pattern and it is our purpose to exhibit that pattern. If any of us choose not to, we call to ourselves the actions of reverse energy. Have you ever seen a vehicle speeding forward and have it suddenly reverse by compaction? You understand. We are going this way. If for some reason we choose not to go that way and our mandate is going that way, it is going to hurt. You may try to stop, but you can choose how to exhibit the mandate. That is your power, also.

When I purposely stepped forward for this interaction, I wanted to state to you these things of Source and energy, but I also wanted to state it to you, my gladness and my strength then lies at your feet. If I said I have purpose here, I have longed for you. My fellows speak true of this in their strange tongue, their chirpings and twitterings.

Let me say the strength of their tongue is the same as yours might be here. The spoken word carried less than the Light that shines from the eyes and the hearts, so then we become as one unit. I lay myself at your feet. I state I am at your service. I state what you need. Call to me and the others will speak. Do not be afraid. It is purposeful. Do not think it to be an imposition. If any of you need action of any sort, it is part of this mission called Earth Healing.

When the Earth becomes whole, when we are concluded, we shall know what we have done, and we shall regale each other with tales of how it was and how it shall be again is another space. These are not war stories. This is the statement that within the spaces and the halls of all the Universes, the finest step forward and their time is to be veiled. That is the simplest way I can say it.

We shall go back to this in the future and we shall say, "Remember when we first really knew what we were doing. We are not saving a planet, we are endorsing the very Source energy in all the Universes of all time. We are saying "God IS". All people are one in action and thought, and we are not saying we cannot allow this to be, we are saying, but, of course, we come from the same source. We shall be as one. This healing time is for all time here forward. This healing time is for all time before now. It is happening that it is on Earth. It could as well be on any other planet, but strong purpose is to release the essence for all people for all time.

So, that is your matter. That is your Beingness. That is your psychological makeup. That is your emotional expression. All of the things that you are are the product of that vocalization energy. If there are things happening to you that you cannot decipher, go back into this, how does this relate to why I am here? It will be much faster. What is this telling me about my role? You will know sooner. It will not be a minor issue. If you think one thing to be of a small nature, you will be very surprised. The smallest issue will be aggrandized into Universal importance. It does not make us more than one person of the masses, it just makes us action. Can you perceive this?

"Yes."

Now, I shall set myself on this chair and you may speak, if you like, about questions that you have. (Kortron is speaking to a group that is meeting at my apartment. Questions are from that group.)

"It used to be that you could fix things, now it seems that it is sometimes better to say nothing. You say that you always will know what to say. I seem to always say the wrong thing, so perhaps quiet is better."

Let's say that perhaps you have the main ingredient, stillness, and if one speaks to you about how they might perceive this, allow let them speak first and then state, "Perhaps, this is how this might work."

"This has happened to me twice recently with people. It is profound."

Yes.

"Their change in their realization . . . they got it. I see what you mean . . ."

Yes, and then you may present it as an option.

"but rather than force, wait until they initiate . . ."

Yes, and then be very free to speak, and yes, if you cannot think to speak from your mind, then be aware that a moment's stillness and a connection will allow the consciousness to speak through your lips. The consciousness is the voice of accumulated wisdom of all times. All that you do is given back to the consciousness. You know this. This is not the voice of God. This is the accumulated voices of all the peoples, all the thoughts, all the planets, everything is contained. This is a great archive.

Consciousness is an intelligent focal energy. Allow that to speak through you. It is very precise. It is very selective. It is what your guidance is. It is what actually provides you with exactly that amount of money to drive that far and you thought it wasn't coming and perhaps you won't make it there, but you do. That is the consciousness working with you. It is involved with trust. It is involved with secure confidence which I just spoke of. When you allow this to speak, you then absolve your guilt reflexes. Your difficulties melt away because it is the voice speaking and allow that to be, and soon you become to know it is trustworthy.

The first time the emotion is to pull forth more of your own wisdoms, but if you practice, you find that the consciousness has more access . . .

"Umhumm. More is always less and less is . . ."

Very often more. Exactly. Yes, very good question. It is a good practice when you have the difficulty of not knowing quite what to say or when, if you just let a moment's silence take and then before you have to ask, clear yourself, close your eyes and say, "I'm thinking."

"People always wonder on Earth if you don't respond immediately."

If they are aware, say that. Say, I'm asking or listening to expand my response and then they know they can do that, too, but sometimes it is much better to have two involved because they can relax, or if you are getting some answers, I can relax for a few minutes, then I'll take charge again. That is the difference when one comes to you and you offer or interject. They have command.

That is what you see so often in those such as I which you may presume to be an overextension of energy. It is supreme confidence, the ability to be what I am and notice others awareness but not be uncomfortable by that awareness. If they choose not to care for me, that is their awareness state. I feel it is not my imposition. I have learned this over many eons of time and practiced it. So have you the ability to be, to not interject, to not impose, but to not give way because we ought. You understand? I AM, YOU ARE need not give way, and to laugh at mistakes. There are no mistakes. There are some unfortunate incidences. (Chuckles)

"I have a question about crystals and I am not sure I have it formed with the words, but I started working with them and selling them about a year and a half ago when they were brought into my shop. I couldn't sleep for about three nights. I finally realized that there was a lot of energy around them. Then I became accustomed to it. I don't feel each crystal like I used to. When I first got them, when I was pricing them or something, I was feeling each crystal and really getting into it. Now I don't, and I also know that they are tools and I have the feeling now that maybe I am giving my power away if I am putting too much energy into the crystals. Do you understand what I am saying?"

Yes.

"I am not sure how to formulate answers to people who come to me in the marketplace. They always ask me, "How do you feel with these crystals and so on and I am not sure I am giving them the right answers. I am giving them my answers and I am not sure that is what they want to hear."

What they want to hear and what they must hear are probably two different things. If you can devise in your private time a way or a leaflet that would help them and perhaps work with someone who also works with stones devise simple explanations that you can hand to them, a very small printed beautiful object on paper. That might assist.

But, also, might I state that the crystals are individuals and you know this. They are personages. They are intelligent intellectual individuals who choose to be here, so they will do much speaking and you may not speak for them, but you must have some simple explanations. May I say the explanations must be in consideration of both parties, both the crystal and the people who are human. Most people who come to you will not view them as intelligent resourceful individuals. You might state, "The crystals are sacred. They carry Light. They are very beautiful." Very simple statements. We are both aware everything is sacred, but for this purpose state, "They are sacred. They are ancient energy. They are helpers."

They are an absolute. They are so independent that they can be without humans. They are volunteering. See, this is what I want you to do. They are available to us when we have high motivation. These are the kinds of things you want to transfer. They will not magnify our evil Intent. They will magnify our clear Intent. If we desire to have better health, a crystal will magnify that by its resonance, its vibrational tone. If we ask it to assist us when we do healing work for others, it will magnify that Intent.

Now, if you talk in those terms, you must also explain, you cannot heal another without their permission. So you want to be aware of how much information they can have. I would suggest it be very, very simple. Perhaps you want to verse yourselves by putting down the simplest phrases and using the same phrases all the time. Otherwise, you are going through this cordiality countless times with many strangers all of whom receive it in their countless ways. You will be very tired of this.

You can say this, "I work with the crystals. I use them, but I work with them because I love them. Here is a sheet to tell you their possibilities."

If they need none of it and you find it crumpled on the floor, that is their business. The crystals that go to those folks who might know nothing . . . they have agreed to it. When you have a shipment that comes to you, it is important to take moments of time to touch each one because your vibration will assist them to do their work. I would suggest, if you choose, to allow celestial energy to come to this specific purpose. Touch each one. It can be very swift. Then they know. Say, "Welcome, it is so good to have you here." It is very important for the line of energy.

It is important for your vegetables. It is important as you mow the grass. It is important in every aspect of your life to open all of the avenues. When one is closed, people of your import, have a backlash energy. When one avenue is closed, there is a stoppage. When you view you from a distance you would see that you would have your central flame as your essence. It radiates in all directions. It goes this far strongly (several feet) and continues. You bathe others in your radiance and when you meditate or when you go to your Intent of purpose and you clarify, in an instant you say, "I AM of Light. I AM God." It goes out further. The Ray is strength.

When you then allow yourself to be utilized for the purpose we have adopted with the crystals, you can take them into your essence and assist their journey and that extends beyond you. When this Being has at any moment a blockage, and let us not say that you cannot forget. You certainly can forget to bless the lawnmower, but the next time you go through the yard say, "Oh". Pat it, talk to it. That devic energy must have your support or it cannot interact properly. When you block that action by purposely denying that, your radiance does not go beyond that.

So, you are becoming beatific. That's where the lessons come in. Many of the strong ones now have substance/residue left from times before and what you need is a healing comprehension, so I will make some body suggestions. You need an amicable massage therapist—very light touch, very light touch—you have a process of releasing toxins. It is very common now with Light bearers of your nature who have human bodies. You are not alone, believe me, it is very common. When then, the body is trying to release toxins and it cannot, it is a very light touch or you will have so many released, you will be in agony.

You also have a substance called chlorophyll on this Earth. You need a great deal of that. All of you do, you need water, clear water to clear the cells. Do not do a crash program. You will be sick. You are being detoxed, but you are having such an access of energy from celestial sources. You are releasing toxins and you have celestial energy there and they are meeting in the middle. You are reaching out for more and you are mired in toxins.

Chlorophyll, however you choose to use it. I am aware on you planet that you have the liquid form. The dark green will help you very much to rid yourself of the toxins. Greens, great cleansing greens. Eat greens from the garden. This is Spring, the beginnng. It makes a statement. Be fresh.

Then you attend to the etheric body. That is your brilliance. You can do that very easily in meditative positions. Stand before the open window and address yourself as brilliance. Just see it. See each of those positions you know of as chakras in tune. You do not have to image anything except crystalline Light, the simplest matter. What you were doing is honoring, cleansing, honoring, cleansing. Do you do exercise?

"Not if I can help it, but I need to do it more."

This is holding you back. This is holding in your body the toxins. The best way for a human body to rid itself of the toxins is perspiration. I am not speaking of the kind where you sit upon a bench in a tight chamber and breathe hot air. I am speaking of the kind where you move your human form in great mobility until the pores open up, until the inner body heat raises, until the inner body heat purges itself. It is artificial to expect that dynamic to happen from external temperature putting yourself through a great hazard, in my opinion. It is very difficult for your cells to adjust to that intense heat, and the fresh air, especially in the morning early, that process of aerobic exercise which purges from the inside out where you can breathe cool air and have it wash about you. You are replenishing the cells with oxygen. You must have oxygen. You must have clear water. This is crystal. You are holding yourself back.

The physical difficulties for people who do not have enough exercise will increase because their bodies can't handle the vibratory changes. You can exercise at any form pattern unless your leg will not move for some reason and then you can flail your arms. Any form can exercise and work into sweat. The body will know. Walking is very, very good exercise. Fast.

"In listening to you, I assume the vibrations will continue to rise. Can you explain a little more about how we can adjust to deal with it?"

Yes. The thing that you most desire is to reach a state of mind whereby you can adjust no matter what is happening and you don't even have to know because your body says, "Now we need to do these things." The basic ingredients of life on any planet manifest out in the forms of that planet. The forms are designed to interact with the planet and the forms must or they cannot live.

When a human species has taken itself away from the Earth energy accessed to the core viability, when a human species has no connection with what you call soil and trees and grasses and water—or limited—this is what most happens. You may think, "Oh, I am connected," but I am saying to you, you are not, because you have to spend quantities of time and it is to your benefit and it can be incorporated into exercise as you call it. It becomes a way of life, you see. When then you act as your body instructs, your body will take care of the adjustments.

Your body may say lie down, you need to lie down . . . three times a day you need to lie down. It will only take ten minutes to balance out the energy. Your body may absolutely demand because you think your head is going to blow off. This is how you are feeling sometimes. It sets up in your inner regions in the cells a vibration that cannot be toned. You must lie down. You can lie on the grass. This is the best or the sand of the beach. This would be very good. Don't lie on big boulders. They are dynamic energy. Grass or sand. You can lie in the dirt if you don't mind getting dirty. Grass is a wonderful transmuting vibration. Very efficient and important.

As then you lie down and you begin to feel the difference, you will feel the energy taking care of itself. It will move out, it will move up and down. It will balance itself. Your body can be submerged into that element refreshed, restored. That is healing. You listen and respond. That is healing.

The other things that take place are that the body dynamics may require more sleep or meditation. It is up to you to design this. Meditation displaces sleep to a certain extent. You will require meditation regularly and in quantity. It is your connection. It cannot be avoided. It is a sense of responsibility to yourself. It will draw you into those modes. If you don't feel well, ask yourself what you are doing. Ask yourself your choices. Ask yourself the importance of you. If you cannot attend to your form as a human being, then something is not functioning appropriately.

As then you have exercise to think about, think about it in terms of moving your energy. It isn't very long but must be very fast at half an hour. If you choose to move more slowly, then you must move longer. Do you follow this? There are the dynamics that must take place. When humans breathe with their nostrils, with their lungs, they breathe in and out a matter of themselves. A matter of air constitutes their physical cell structure. It is like eating. If you breathe air from inner city turbulence, you will be turbulent in nature. If you breathe the air from a construction site with much fumes, you will be sickened. This is very common knowledge, but many still do this practice. They breathe the air of the cities and they do not breathe the air of the freshness of the trees and the waters and the country.

The waters and the country and the trees, this is your cell structure. Be very aware the Earth is you. Never humans have superimposed upon the planet those things like cities and highways and zones where pollutants have been released. This is not your cell structure. Living it and breathing it, you shall become that, you shall become sickened. The original planet is your structure. As you exercise then, you want to breathe that structure.

If you can choose to be in a place where you walk high in the mountains or hills several times a week and breathe those airs several hours at a time, you shall become that. It shall become your way and you will be nurtured. Then you will not have to know if it is six months or if it is going to be an explosion of Mt. St Helena or if the California coast will tremble or if there is a war in Afganistan, it will not matter. You are fully functioning. You are endorsed. You are at post. When you are at post, you act and you know when you must meditate, or send energy, or become available to others. It is not your job to monitor the world condition. Just be aware of this.

You need not even know what is going on with it. It is your job to take care of your body, to have joy, to laugh as much as possible and to act when you are requested. This I shall expand upon. When you are asked to act, you shall know it. Somehow you shall be notified to do this thing. It may to become to this place so that we may talk. It may be to sit in front of the computer terminal, get orders and state, "I AM ready." It may be assist another to become more full. It may be to walk in the forest at high altitude and exchange energies. The forest needs you, too.

I am telling you that the society perceives the possibility of what we are all seeking of, but the society does not have the wholeness to understand. The society is trying to draw itself up at the same time that they are designing greater weapons. It is a novel situation. It is again a conflict between those who would create and heal whether you want it or not, and those who would destroy. Take yourself out of this system. Take yourselves out of the destructive systems as much as possible.

You will know the systems I speak of. They will make a statement to you. As much as possible without being arrested, please take yourself out of the systems. If it is requested that in the name of peace people come forth, you can go and become, but leave before they arrest. Let those who would choose to be there at that moment be arrested. It is not your job. It proves nothing, and is a big headache. Then you are off post. As then you take yourself out of the systems, you need not even know what is happening in your town in terms of the disasters. You will hear about them sooner or later.

When you hear of something that is unusual, if it seems to fit the pattern that we are all speaking of, you can observe it and say, "Ah!" In other words, do not go to the offensive. Do not go down into pity. Be aware of the actions that are taking place. Release them into glory. Be capable of stating yourself in the midst of catastrophes. The only way you can do that is to become so whole that you know yourself in confidence. You are in position and when others ask you for your help, say, I can't do any more. I am doing all that I know I am supposed to do. You need explain no further. You need give no money. You can send prayers to all the Universes. That is your work.

"So when people get into certain situations, say a heroin addict, they have chosen that, correct? Then why would it be my place to pray them out of it?"

Let us say that in your nature of being, you can exhibit to them the concern of the cosmos. What this means is you have the responsibility, the privilege, the right, the possibility to send them the golden Light. This is the council's consent. The golden Light allows them to become unto their fullest possibility. In other words, you attach them. You are saying, "Here is what I can give you. It is straight from God. It is all you need. I trust you to know what to do with it."

The war against drugs will not be successful because it is being approached from the wrong vibrational tone . . . a war. Healing aspect will come from the examples, voices, thoughts, and actions from those who come to bear Light in truth, and the way that they emanate their vibration. You cannot emanate your vibration in purity and negate all of the efforts. That is why you must attend to your own personal bodies. If one point comes in this conversation and they say, "I cannot sit any longer. I must go out outside", and it is honesty, it is not stating unto another I don't like it, it is saying I must go out into greater air.

Questions from Joyce—"May I ask two questions? I have had a lifetime of history of bad headaches, and now, all of a sudden, I get bad headaches, and then all of a sudden, they are gone without any pills and I think that is a different type of thing. I want to ask about that—but I also want to ask this, I am very aware of my job, what I came here to do. You also spoke about the resonance. If we leave a certain area, we have lost part of the resonance. If we go to another area, they have their own resonance. I find it very difficult at times to live in the city. I am not a city person, never have been. If I went a few miles away into the hills, would I have jarred the resonance, so to speak?"

Your guidance is saying to you right now, it is time to move out of this vibration.

"Yes."

You have very strong guidance. Trust it.

"So then what I need will be provided. I don't have to have money and all that kind of thing. Something will happen and I will have what I need?"

59

The headaches are because your tension mounts, because you are an Arcturian and you are implanted in this body, sometimes it is difficult to cope. And there is a tendency in many human beings to allow tension to mount. I am aware of this. It is a common disorder and you know this.

"Yes."

It is an appointed time coming when you can release those issues, and it is by your appointment to your confidence and your trust, and then you will find literally as you sit in the most common position in the same stated place that you sat before now, three hundred times, you had tension and now you have no tension. You will feel that you have not the need to have the tension. That is the difference. Then you can choose. And when you feel it mount, tension closes down the cells. It is a muscular action that states, "I am on guard, I am on duty." It is a combative disposition. All body parts state unto it and with the head, because it is very important, it is the very barest of cell structure. There isn't much there, there is a lot of bone, not to exhibit that it is empty, there is just not much there but bone to allow muscular viability.

There are several things you can do, one is to pay attention to the things I have spoken of, and as you come into tension, allow it to melt away. Say, "I do not have to be in this combative position. I am being what I am in truth. I am in my power." As then that exhibits to you, you will notice more and more that you are able to let go of that process. When you massage your head, when you allow these cells to open and expand, you are loving yourself and you are stating, "Now we can relax." Now we can let go of your headaches. The headaches are not from the inside of your skull, they are from the outside of your skull. It is a very tight band of energy. When it tightens even more, there is no room for approving energy. When you close off approving energy, you suffer. You take away that which is the Source of flowing energy.

(In later years, I found this to be absolutely true. As I came into my own power KNOWING that I AM God espressing to my highest and best and I am into my own power, the headaches magically went away. How much less pain I would have had to endure, had I learned that lesson sooner!)

Question is from one who owns a crystal shop and who makes sacred jewelry. "You are saying to take care of ourselves, but I think if I do that, I am being selfish. I think I should be helping others rather than myself."

If you think you have to help others, you are indicating that they are not appropriate in their mode. Let us state that perhaps your job is to offer, and in your wisdom, you must restate your view of yourself. To take care of yourself is extending your energy field so that it is balance, it is whole, and you are healthy and the ability to send the strength that you send constantly, whether you know it or not. You transmute constantly. Your body cannot do that successfully, and that is why ones get sick unless it is balanced.

So, it assures you and you must then understand that it is all right. So that is what you are dealing with, this guilt. This is a refinement. But also let us state that rather than offering help, you are offering what you are. You are offering your silvers and crystals. You are offering the designs. It is your job, and with it offer sustenance of your vibration and the speaking. It comes together. You are literally living that which you must be. So you need never have guilt about doing more of it. You are doing plenty. You will be offered opportunities to be among the people many times, many places. This is when you extend the energy.

When you are not doing that, you must receive. You cannot do this all the time. There won't be anything left. It will come out of your cell structure. You must receive so that you are refurbished so that you are a clear energy. It is very difficult for human beings to sustain. There is a refinement of the process of the social system that says, "You cannot be for yourself, you must be for all others." This is a misnomer. It is a misunderstanding of the concept of unconditional love. Unconditional love allows others to be themselves.

"How do you allow yourself to love other people unconditionally? I notice I love people if they are doing what I perceive they should be doing and when they are not doing that, I am holding back as a way of punishing them, not really wanting to do that, but I am noticing that is what I do?"

61

Yes, this is a good point. I think perhaps it is not to love them, but to become love. You desire to become love, then you can by actions bring Light into your being and this will be discussed later. So now I must go from you, not too far, you can call on me if you need me. Bon Voyage— you are on a journey, you know.

Joyce speaks—Kortron is an incredible being. I am so in sync with his energy. As with all Beings of his demeanor, he is able to be/do many things at the same time. I left this gathering having been forever imprinted by a discussion about Focus and Intent, knowing, or rather remembering, that the most powerful force in the Universe is powered by the use of Focus and Intent which is the key to manifesting or creating anything that we do. I have subsequently learned that this is what powers everything through the Universes whether it is on the starships or planets or stars or here in the Earth plane.

I went back, listened to this tape, and discovered there was nothing on the tape having to do with Focus and Intent finally realizing that while I was listening to the above channeling, I was at the same time involved in an overlay that was given me personally by Kortron teaching me the importance of Focus and Intent. It was so clear to me and so intensely given that I have it taught it in every one of my classes and used it in my life from that time forward, yet there is nothing on tape that I had ever had the discussion!

At the time, this discovery blew me away. Today, I am well aware that there is nothing impossible with these Beings. I am so ever grateful and so humbled that these powerful ones have come to be in discussion with me.

At another time, I discussed this phenomenon with Gayl, the channel. She retrieved the information that Kortron had been a parent of mine in some lifetime as well as an instructor/guru of mine probably in a subsequent lifetime. Whatever it is, I have a real connection with Kortron and some of the greatest learning of this lifetime has come from him.

Chapter 5

Anna of Ashtar 5

"Hello, Anna."

I have been known to much of yourself in the past before now. I am come into new ways than before, when you knew me, but I am well acquainted with your work here. I have come a long way in this transmission. It is not of the sort as Spirit in habitation, but as you know now, we can code in to the tracking device that is called form and now you have the unilateral subdividing channel that you have been equipped with before you came to this nation.

This allows a subdividing of the energy currents that are specified for you and indicated to be for you for your transmitting and receiving, not to be confused with another's. Significantly, we can code in and out to specific individuals. And here as you see, I am a component of energy extending. Thus, when you choose to code in to me, I can receive the equivalent of your energy extension into fact, in form. Should you choose this, you can extend enough energy to me to be upon this ship in your form.

"I could?"

Yes, now you can do this now. You have been coded long before here.

"Every human . . . does every human have this?"

No, no, ground crew has this. The way we speak of 25% . . .

"So, Anna, simply by calling to you and seeing myself there with you, is that how we do this?"

This is a way. This is to promote ground crew ingenuity and integrity, integrity meaning to integrate with fleet crew. So, you call upon me, calling Anna of Ashtar 5, Bitterroot Squadron. I signal in, Haelegram call Joyce upon Earth. This gives me your coding name, Haelegram. It is what you have been, what you came with, and Joyce tells me where you are because I know you. You are a station. You did not know this, did you?

"No."

Ha! You are a station now. You are a receiving station for stellar transmission. This can allow me by your coding name, you signal in to the fleet that this aspect of your existence opened up.

"OK."

You are recalling and taking responsibility. You came here from Arcturus on a ship. I tell you what it looked like. This will help you recall.

"All right."

It is silver as in this effect, very swift, but the luminous skin is not of metal as you know, though you might say more pewter color.

"OK."

Glowing . . . also as what you call pewter as of this and with what you call glass is here all along.

"OK."

So, it is a graceful fish object. This mission upon this ship had accorded you access to the earth dimension, so when you left Arcturus, you knew the mission, and it was to be coming to Earth, but you spent several centuries observing Earth, watching, knowing exactly what to do and transmitting that information back to your planet, occasionally going back to your planet. You have spent much time upon the ships. This particular ship is the specific object of your endeavor and it awaits still in the atmosphere and you can also return to that ship. The stellar name is Aaschjan. You are Haelegram of Aaschjan.

It is a ship that is not a mother vessel but rather travels between.

"I understand."

It still does this service upon the ways of the fleets. You have much access to these as soon as you stimulate the memory banks. This pattern, this mode that you perceive is not mine, what I will comprehend to you will be my way, plus your way, plus others. You came not as a functioning mechanized machine. When I say you are ground station, that is only an applicable term. It is not to tell you that you have a device of robot-like consistency. It is not so. It is only that you now are sensor device for the ships.

"Partly by Intent because that is what we want to do."

Exactly. Exactly. You came prepared. Therefore, you programmed yourself in a pattern to be in accord. If you had programmed yourself to resist this, nothing we could do would change this. So, we had agreement before you came this would be, and others also.

I have spoken also with one named Tenaso. She also can receive. So, we have other stellar connections coming to you in the future. Again, not so familiar as I shall be, nor you to your ship, but other ways and this is well. You will learn all of the ways.

The ships are not of etheric form. They are each carrying the populous of a planetary system that they came from. The etheric form needs no such vessel, and although you can think the ships are etheric, it is that they are of a molecular structure that is so fine that it cannot be seen. It is indeed of a structure, atomic molecular structure that can exist and does, and carries its inhabitants. It is not of your way as you see it here. It is of your former way.

The ship that you came from from Arcturus, Mother Ship, is of a very subtle design, and yet very efficient as to be able to plunge through the atmosphere and out and through the time dimensions swiftly, so swiftly as to disassemble its molecular structure and move forward into another dimension. This is not a category of speaking for now. That is for a later knowing, but I tell you how advanced you come from. And you have others of your nature about. Some will be coming in forms speaking. They will come about. You will begin to know.

The empowerment you seek, Haelegram, is that you know everything you are. That is what you seek. That is what you choose to hear. That is what you desire, the connection. I am telling you one signal will heal this that you seek. It is to not care if it occurs.

"I figured that."

It is to tell you that you are so complete that you cannot deny what you are, but you deny what you are by being too intent upon the search, because you are already where so many try to go, so you block the flow. It is coming very soon within a month that you will truly realize that it doesn't matter because what you are is complete. No matter what else is added, you are complete, and then the last layers will fall away . . .

"OK."

. . . and the complete communications may be stated.

"What bothers me . . . and I am getting through a lot of stuff, but still dealing with the responsibility. See, I feel a responsibility to all of you. I feel a responsibility to Holanea and his people who want to speak to me that I feel that I can't do this, and then I get upset because I can't, because then I block it."

I tell you why we let you be this way—because you had to experience the more guttural expression called form. They are most painful expression of your power. Because you had been so capable and so powerful, you carried this, you knew it, but in order to understand form, you could not be expressing this power. You would sweep ones away, sweep them under the rug.

Now, you have known these ways and you can see indeed that the struggle to know more inhibits the knowing. That is something we had to let you be with. Now we can tell you there is no more time for this. You don't have to do this any more, but it is truly so much trust that you don't care. Because the individual soul draws down experience and when there is so much struggle to know it means then that the Spirit can't just trust that they know. Do you see?

"Yes."

So that is allowed to go through the struggle. So, now you have abundance of information. It is of clerical nature. We give you over and over now new information, this categorizes what you know and you remember in an instant. It is so that you can say, "Yes, it is true, I do know this," so now we verify for you and tell you that you can come to a pattern. It is of stating what I am is complete. I can wait.

Then Holanea can come and speak because the patterns must be very fine to speak through, so you see?

"Yes."

And the struggle makes denser patterns. So we had to give you time.

Now the activation of the device allows you to receive the energy and transmit and you will begin to feel the pulsations of the way the ships transmit. Even if your brain cannot quite uncode yet, you will know, and when you speak in your thoughts, we will pick it up.

You can directly address me, "Anna of Ashtar 5 Bitterroot Squadron, this is Haelegram Joyce on Earth."

"Is the Ashtar symbol in the <u>Celestial Rays</u> book accurate?"

It is complicated a slight amount . . .

"Sort of."

but essentially. It is the determination of each communication then to recreate. 'Tis similar. You see, each fleet has their own symbol, and so all come together to make a similar symbol. Do you see?

"Yes, I am also . . . maybe I shouldn't ask this in your position, Anna, but I am going to ask it anyway. Why am I so attracted to the White Brotherhood materials. Is that part of what we did on the ship, is that part of it? Is it both on the ship and on Earth?"

Yes. White Brotherhood is an effective symbology to those upon Earth, but White Brotherhood is of all standards everywhere.

"That's a help."

It is to say a coding or tracking system for those upon Earth for the Universal wisdoms, so it is the Universe speaking and many can move in and through this energy pattern symbolically stating, "We are of the White Brotherhood", but it is truly a Universal creation, the Brotherhood. It is of a different nature than some can speak of.

Now, to embody the words of my message as we say that I am Anna, Commander of this ship I am upon, and I tell you many things about myself in the future. It is not for training nor for playing that we do this, but rather to understand better the tracking device that you are becoming. So, it is to you that I will transmit saying we are having communication difficulty. Let us test this, for I am not the training agent here, but rather I can speak to you, and in this process tell you a few things about myself.

This allows me to be extending my range and my reality unto the Earth peoples. Then, at the appropriate time, we have immediate contact. When there is need, we can hear. So this, in a term, is your training device. I am not your trainer. I am your friend, your comrade, and we are beginning the signal systems.

"Is there a specific place or time that you want me to be to make this better?"

There is a way. If you would designate a time per day, perhaps towards the evening, this is a good for me because of your atmosphere being clear. You can designate shortly before going to bed. We do not want to inundate your energy. Do you feel any undo energy at this time?

"No."

Then my tracking is sincere and I can complete because I know I have not offended you. This is also part of what we do together. If the major ones can accept the vibrations and receive and transmit, then we can begin the adjustments with these ones who know what they are doing. There is no question. I know this. I know when I come to you and say, "This is Anna of Ashtar", even though we do not meet upon the ground of your nation, you know we are one.

"Yes."

And it is well and I will not offend you and we will make refinements, as another awakening one may not feel the same. This is very important work.

"Oh, I understand how important."

We establish the links, so we are being a part of the communications network. And as you have achieved this many times before as Chief of Staff for the Linguistics Division of the Arcturian Fleet, you have accomplished exactly what we are doing in a different mode and from a different level because before you worked upon the ships.

"Linguistics then and dyslexic now!"

Aw, this is only to displace what you do not need. Yes, we program a little bit for you to get rid of . . .

"It keeps me humble, too!"

It does, it does. I have experienced this. I came upon this way once before several times ago. I could not speak. I had to learn this vocabulary. I could not transmit the proper vibrations to use this vocabulary. Then I learned. Now I am still learning much more, faster, I learn. You will, too. You are relearning the pattern and the speech. It will be different than it has been here on earth. You will learn more by Intent to speak.

"Great!"

Yes. I have service to the one Source that is the same as yours. It is to bring Peace and Abundant Life upon the nation called Earth. It is to this planet that I am drawn, directed, and in this work I promise my way shall be here for the duration, as you all say. Can tell you as we began, this work will be continuing. For right now, the major focus is the communications link up so that all along these great mountains and coast, we have the major ones hearing, being able to receive without distortion and without discomfort.

"So then, I was more or less, sent out here from Bozeman, wasn't I? It wasn't just . . ."

Ah yes. Ah yes. The great Ashtar, himself, has located the ground crew upon the spaces necessary. You will see much, much more. You will have communications, but I tell you to trust that it will come.

"I trust."

Not one negative motive is coming from yourself or to yourself.

"It just seems like it takes so long, but for you, it must seem even longer."

I have been upon the ship twenty seven times of your years here about Earth, seven times have I not been exactly here, but traveling. Twenty times I have been about your Earth. I am not of nervous countenance, excitability. It does not matter where I serve, although I sometimes tend to come and go in my energy to return unto my planetary ways.

"Are you . . . were you also from Arcturus?"

I am not. I am from another stellar system soon to tell to you in a way you can understand. I now have an abundance of information to give you as you can receive, and it is not a mode of training, but rather interaction. And as we are speaking, as the communication is being set, it will not be technical to say, "Do you receive me over and out?" It will be to speak people to people. So, I have things to tell you and you me . . . dialogue, conversation, much as a phone line to you, but not to me . . . to me living complete so then you will also be come to me living, complete.

First, you will be able to receive much like a phone line and I will tell you how to begin. Later, you will be able to release your energy to see the ship, to come to it to extend your energy along the pattern of Light that I beam to you. The way the communication can work is that through my system, I can project a beam of Light that will be like the technology of the phone line, much more powerful, coming in to you here. That is why sometimes it is too strong, it is too much frequency then we can experiment until it is right. Then when you say, "It is too much right now", then I will lessen. It is never to be of discomfort.

Then as you are practicing with this, eventually you will feel yourself rise on the beam of Light and you will see, and become onto the ship and I will know and I will welcome.

Now, the best way to accomplish this is to set a time in your thinking. Go into the space, allow about ten minutes meditation. You are away about twenty minutes for the preparation of the form. This will be the first step. Do not expect instantly to speak. It is a preparation of the form and you will experience movements of energy. The velocity or the frequency rate will be raised and this we will give to you, bring to you specifically. It is not a part of your coding to be left in the actual rate. It is a transfer rate we bring and all of the ones receive this who are knowing.

"Is it important to hold . . . will the crystals help raise the vibration if I hold crystals?"

It is to be spoken that you must have what is called rose quartz. This will help to balance and just hold . . . just hold. It will help to balance. That is all. The transfer rate is to bring you into a higher frequency faster. This is what the other peoples will go through, but they must be abundantly cared for and this will be part of your work. As you go through this transfer rate, you will literally feel your form make adjustments. It will seem at times, perhaps, to be uncentering, but if it is at the end of a day, it does not harm you. It is not to be physical pain, but it definitely can be physical adjustment. Notice, as you are having vibrations of higher frequency, then the device will allow you to begin tracking easier and easier.

You are never to begin to take all kinds of miscellaneous transfer of energy. It is to be directly channeled through Anna at this time. You will be given notice when there is a broader range. If, ones somehow come into your frequency, it is by accident or perhaps from another stellar system that is beginning to send their vibratory message into Earth and they are doing this to reassure and to say, "We are out here and we love you." They will want to do this. It is not time for you, otherwise, you will be much confused. If that should occur, merely state, "It is not appropriate at this time. I have not the method to receive you. Do not transmit to me at this moment. I only communicate with Anna. Repeat. It is not the time." At that same time, put a golden shield over your head. This reflects back the message.

I choose that as you come to the meditative state that you do the act called 'Bringing down the Light' and this makes the statement, or some other method that is equally efficient to you. As you begin the interaction, you can begin the communication and that is to state, "Coding in Haelegram. This is Joyce of Earth." Your coding in only means that is your vibrational frequency from another time from the ships. It is a partial signal. The complete signal then is 'Joyce of Earth'. So you see you have been 'Halegram Joyce of Earth' and you release the vibratory. It is to you static. It will be picked up by either one of my crew members or myself. It will come on our panel and I will answer.

We have quite a large ship. It may take me a moment to come into the communications panels. And then, one will always be at the panel and can answer, and I will come and we will converse. So, if you feel an answer, that is well, don't be a-feared. We will pick you up when we get there.

There is no harm to you at all. It is part of your way. You have known this many times. As your body and others begin to more and more diffuse into Light, you will feel the lift lighter and lighter, and it is an urgent part of your mode to become more of this way. This is what I say to be frequency transfer so that you are coming higher into these levels. Do you see this?

"Yes."

Your form will not disappear, but the molecular structure will become lighter and lighter. Now, I will withdraw, the panel is being closed, and, if you ever need to contact us, remember the panel can be opened, your frequency will be picked up as a signal rising and we will immediately open and make the link.

"Thank you."

You are welcome. We also have connection with the one named Tenaso and when she begins this and you can share. Do not be a-feared that nothing will happen. Everything will happen, so let it go through its levels, first the form-integration, and then the training. When you have gone through the form-integration and the change in the molecular structure is felt by you, you will know when the time has come to literally begin to send the signal. Then we will begin the training time. That is more complex, but it will be well. You will remember much, very fast and, at the right point, you can output your energy and interject it into the capsule that you came upon. You can go back through the time element and become the form that you were and see where you went when you arrived and that will release all your memory bank.

Your key is not to doubt it and thus you will not struggle. It is slipped upon you like a silver gown. So, now I have many things to do. I do not stay long in one place.

"Well, thank you for all this time."

You are quite welcome. Hummm. I embrace you and I give you love.

"I return it."

Abba

I am indeed called Abba. It is in your framework that I choose to be called Abraham, but not in Biblical concept. Do not be in reference to me as anything you have ever known. I am here to speak upon your way that you may know me. I have come from a multi-dimensional forestat. This makes unto your way a presentation of elements that is not presentable to your form, a forestat being that which is ephemeral in form and yet solidified in a molecular structure that is compatible to the form that I am.

As you may perceive what I am, you may not see me. I vibrate at a pattern that is far higher than your perception, you can foretell, and yet I am of a nature that is of substance as surely as you are. As some have come from a forestat that is compounded of molecular structure similar to your Earth and has yet not congealed into actual form, I have compatibility with you but not structural sameness, and I cannot quite live in your dimension. Therefore, I come and go, come and go, that the nurturing may continue that I must manifest for myself.

As you would perceive, I have in my compoundment of energy a manner that is mostly similar to yours in this way that I address you, but in stuff composition not, but still I endeavor to cross the boundaries so that you may see we are in essence the same, essence meaning the distillation of our form and character to be a match in the chemistry point. If you were me to be compounded into your essence, I would match you, but I cannot be compressed. It is distasteful to me, also.

And although I come from a force that would be similar in composition, it is not in actual mode. I can move about my planet as you could move through the water of your composition here. I have a molecular structure that is aligned much as yours might be—front to back, up or down, side to side very similar. It is I that is seen frequently streaking across your vision as you have an ephemeral apparition, as you might say. I have not stayed long at a time, although the endurance factor is rising.

As I can be a component to restore your sensibilities when you have been rattled as you say, I am coming about much because I have the exact parallel in essence. I come about to say that I can stay awhile and apply my theory to you, my restorative quality, because we are the same, but my compression limit being rather low at this point, I cannot stay long. As you rise in your vibrational plane, as I can ply longer to my theory here, I then adjunct to you more and more and stay unto your ways as do my fellows.

You may wonder why we would attempt to do this. When you are coming from Earth stature and into higher vibrations, you may wonder why would we attempt to keep this balance for you. It is because you cannot withstand the vibrations of your own mode. That is why we give you substance to become with, and as I, Abba or Abraham, there are others of my way coming to match with major Light Workers in their rebellion, their rising up. This allows you to be more of substance than you have been, but yet to go more into the Light at the same time so that you see, we are literally balancing you as your rise. We have found that this is particularly applicable to those rising along the coast, because the waves of energy are so strong coming off the ocean. You can perceive that as the rising energy breaks off the coast of California, all others will be affected dramatically. As you could not be literally grounded unto your own ground, we will ground you unto your essence. This is the role that we play.

We come from a multi-dimensional factor that is not of your comprehension, but yet you can feel and thus comprehend our integrity within your forms, so then it becomes less important to understand exactly how we are literally to focus in and try to perceive it. Less important is that you have a scenario and we feel ourselves to be friends, companions, and thus we go forward.

I cannot comprehend literally how form here can survive. It would seem to me it would be compressed into nothingness. Thus, I see that the struggle for survival upon this planet is comparative to the amount of compression. The amount of compression is intensified by the density of the individual thinking and then the individual thinking will be compressed even more by the vibrations which will come. This for me is very hard to comprehend and it is in this way that I speak to you.

I am sure that it is hard for you to comprehend how I may not be compressed and still think and speak. It is so that your integrity of mind will follow you when you have no use for form longer and it is that your speech will also, if you choose to display in such a way.

And so I tell you that we are all very much alike although the essence combination that we have is rare. Your chemical molecular structure could be distilled unto mine. And that is fascinating to me because it was not comprehended to be just so in the beginning. It just happened. So now we have a major role here upon this Earth allowing us to be about the ones who have come into major understanding and assisting much keeping the strength at its highest value.

The inland ways will not be so dramatic as the coastal ways. The reason is that the waters will wash away masses of shoreline, and this will be traumatic for the peoples. On the inland ways, the value of the vibrations will be abrupt at times, but still there will not be the trauma attached. So, there will be more need upon the coastline for our messengers and these shall come about frequently and to state, "We are present and we can fill the need for many once we adapt." (Remember this was channeled in 1988 and we have done much work since then. Latest reports tell us that the coasts of California and Oregon will not be compromised.)

I am not sure how long I will need to adapt. I have tried at least five times in twelve days to come about and it is improving, but I have not adapted, so I must concur somehow into a vibratory plane that will not allow compression to my form. I am challenged by this. I accept this. I would tell you these things early that you would know of our attempt to assist you and that we feel confident that this will suffice. We will be able to assist you.

To tell you this now, I want you to know that those major Lightworkers will not be abandoned into the vibrations as to cause and effect, but rather nurtured in every element that can be found, and this is one. And there are other ways. It is your own cognizance of your need. To be abundantly clear, keep the vibrations of your spaces high, so clear that you may sufficiently nurture yourselves. Keep your ways unto the woods. Keep the times away that you need from others . . . all that has been stated, and thus, in addition to that, we feel quite capable of coming to you, surrounding you with the essence of your sameness to insure your soundness. This makes you capable of more, and allows you more freedom to sustain yourself as the Earth herself gives up of her reason for her knowingness which will be disrupted in these times. The Mother, herself, will have inundation. It will not be so clear to her of her stability.

When it is done, she will resume her mode, but it will seem to some, the very surface of the Earth lacks the gravitation she was. Thus this is our way with you. We cannot stay long now, but we have come five or six of us to be specific with you here now and as we have abundantly assured you, now we shall go. We are learning of your joking way and we say unto you, that we are most glad to have a laughing part of how you be.

And I ask not that you perceive me as any other but your friend, and as the days coming up when you may need our essence to be with yours, call upon us by name first Abraham, then Laka, than Solon, then Frisoe and then Tularay. And we shall come when it is more convenient for us to stay longer and not inundate you. We will make you aware, but we will not need to speak. We will just say, "This is how we are. This is how we feel." And then shall be friends.

And now I shall say, "Thank you."

"Thank you."

You are quite welcome.

Channel and Joyce speaking—Be sure to ground.

"Where were they from?"

Whew!

"I would have liked to have asked them some questions."

My head was just . . . this beanie was just vibrating.

"He's come before. He's with me a lot."

Whereas I have one that signals in over here, he is right here. He first signaled in as Abba, then told me he was Abraham, but not the Biblical concept.

Chapter 6

Halcyvar and Hatonn

And now I give grace to you upon this land called Earth and I bless you and I receive you well into my memory for I am one not of your way and I tell you how I am. I come to you in the form of a molecular structure that to you can be called extension and expenditure of energy. It is a form I give to you that allows an animation of this structure that is agreeable to this format of speaking.

Do not be ambivalent about the way that I may seem. It is here to show you I am not of your way. I am of a mode that is like to you called gelatinous. I have a mode of life that is aquamarine to your thought structure being of a way that might float expediently rather than stride. I have a space upon a starship that is not far from your household. I come in this way upon the manner of Ashtar, the great Lord and Commander of all the fleets. I tell you this that I am to be upon your way many times before.

Do not say to my name as to the way I may pronounce it, but I will tell you what to call me. You cannot say my name. There is no way. It is not in your language. Yet, I say to you that I can be known as Halcyvar. Try to say it the best way you can and you will come close to what I can be called, truly.

Halcyvar is a far cry difference from your way. I am to know this. I have been here to study the species called human for some times before this, and yet I not allow myself to come upon the form called Earth because I desire not to be noticed. So, expediently as might be caused, I have not a way that is more efficient to yours. (Chuckles)—I might be called a jellyfish upon your shores. Had they found me, I know not what they might have done. There, I find this most amusing as you see human forms have intriguement for me, also.

I cannot perceive how you might stand and stride around. I have not a way to understand the structure of a form so upright and stalwart and to actually be able to climb and run. (Chuckles). I have not the mode and yet I perceive I might notice more in the future. Perhaps I will understand. Now, you see we have something in common of understanding of each other.

Let me tell you I have Ashtar 12 which is not so far from you here above your city called Sa-lem, and I like very much the mode we have designed to speak. I might find that I can communicate with you directly, because I have the signal point of your tower. Do you notice? Ha . . . so . . . We have erected a tower for you upon the small land in the middle of the water. It is etheric to your neighbors, but do not say it is just so molecular in structure, yes, and it be thus and it be grounding in to the nature of your planet and it is very, very extended. Thus, we can signal into your tower and thus to yourselves very articulately.

Do not say that to empower you I have come, although it is part of the game that we will play as we move along this path together. I come now to acquaint you with my way and what I am and you to say what you are. Although I may say that I have watched much, so you do not have to tell me much at all. I know this as I have programmed into you before now.

As you know, you have an installation in form, a quadrapel, it is called to me, and it is a significant advancement over those that we have used in past years, years being gilleniums from you. This is a way that you were patterned that you might speak so clearly to the fleets from whence you came. Many have such a manner they do not know, but soon they will find it because it will be stated to them, and through the voice or through their mind will come the acknowledgment that they are indeed from the fleets that brought them to this land and enabled them to receive into flesh.

This is the way of the 25% that knoweth now what they are. They are not of this landscape, and many would be perceiving that they did look like me at some time in the future if you feel a mode to be thus. Often the dancer . . . then they can equate more to what I am.

As you would perceive, I have not known your land so long, but now coming about, I am well acquainted fast and I can speak of this I see so eloquently as to say to you, I know what it is you be now. I see. I cannot land here but I can understand more and more to tell you something. As I be with you, your Intent feeds me vastly. I am knowing so fast that I am 1000% beyond when I could come. This is your way, too. You can advance so fast as to be quickly, fastly beyond the mode of Earthly. It is your way inherited and it can just be. You can say, "Oh," and be so, so fast.

Now, I tell thee that I be on a ship that is, how would you say diaphanous in character, quite mobile and etheric to be seen but not, into a dimension of vibration that is equal to none that you have here. Even to describe, I cannot say, but it is to be known more and you will see these ways that I describe to you. And, the atmosphere within the ship to be that of mine own character and nature so that I can move about through it without harm to me.

There is a way that I extend to you which is of energy vacuum not to leave my form, but to extend my spiritual individuality and here thus to speak so efficient as this. It can be seen much will be done on this planet that will show you what we are. And even if you saw us then, there would be no fear, no harm because we have met so, and the thoughts would say to you as clearly as these words. So now that we have said what I am, let me be unto you in your way and to ask you if you have suffered from the vibrations now tonight. At this time, do you feel thus?

"Not as much."

Too much is it now? To tell me so I can withhold.

"No, not as you are speaking. I had a pain in my head most of the day."

Ah, this is beforehand. Now is well.

"Yes."

And to you?

Tenaso speaking—"Now is well."

And to you? You were not upon this way. I know of this.

Channel's husband—"I didn't have any discomfort."

Now we know and the connection is made. When you perceive this, make the statement clearly. "Ashtar 12. This is Haelegram." (This is your coding.) You can say your name, also, for we know you by Earth name, Haelegram Joyce. "Code Haelegram", (this is your old name) and as you speak, we will pick you up. "The vibratory input is too much for me. Please lower the frequency."

And you, thus, haaa, such a name so close to what you have, Tenaso, "Code name Tenaso, I have too much frequency input. Please lower."

This is very efficient. It is heard. Even the Intent if you want to practice. Intent precedes thought, precedes action and that is what you are teaching much. As you perceive it is not appropriate, you can send the Intent. It will be coded and lowered and those of Earth frequency who cannot stand, or understand, will appropriately come into their modes for we can adjust the plate so that you are more suited. We can make the adjustment for you so that it is more suited.

So now, you are coded in, and you have help in however you proceed. If you act upon this, then it can be stated that you have become a portion of the ground crew. The ground crew is spreading. All those who alighted and now come into knowing, this is the ground crew. They are being prepared for the work ahead. So many, many things will happen, be coming to you.

Do not be a-feared of any. There is nothing coming that is not appropriate. There is nothing coming that is not of the mode that it should be.

For now I say to you that I have exhausted my energy transfer and I must be going now aback into my way, but I have not ways that are so difficult for you to understand nor so different from you that we can't be friends. So we will be linguistically speaking many ways as our language will be able to transfer into other modes fastly. We will not need this. We will be speaking in many other thought patterns. You will be programming yourselves by your choice for the work ahead.

I ask that you each request that you have special sequence with Ashtar's peoples. That makes a mode complete, that agreed we can be in the great and divine circle, coming from the Source of all times, the great Lord of One. I appreciate (slower) and deeply thank you for this interaction. So-na-te.

Channel—You want to ground by breathing down into the earth three times.

Hatonn

The following is a reading done by Gayl in my home for a friend of mine's son in 1987. It gives the clearest description of a starship that I have read anywhere, and for this reason is included in this information.

Hatonn is the Commander of the Intergalactic Fleet from Americus, which is the planet that my friend, Tennie, known to the fleets as Tenaso, comes from. From what we can discern, Americus is not in the Milky Way Galaxy, but rather is part of another star system.

Hello to you. I am the Commander of the Intergalactic Fleet of Americus. My name is Hatonn, and the way I speak is not like yours, but here we have the transfer point—(speaking of the channel) As I would come into your seeking, or your asking, I can then come in on an energy wave from the starship called Molanya, and I will be speaking of the starship to you. I will tell you who I am, where I am from and what I am doing.

I am first of all of the Divine manifestation as you are. I have another form which is not so different from yours, but is different. As I have seen my way upon the galaxies, I now perform a certain status. Status is not to be confused with levels or rank. Status is merely a position. I, being Commander of the Intergalactic Fleet, am from Americus, a planet not in your solar system, not so far away if you can travel on Light, but very, very far if you cannot.

These are theories that will be applied to you in the future, my friend. It will come to you. It is known that you are of the fleets. You come from the fleets, onto this earth life. It is why you are interested. I repeat that I am of the Divine application. This I wish you to clearly understand as your curious mind probes the scientific applications, know that we serve the same Source, the Light, All That Is. It is called God on Earth. In my way, it is merely the Light Being.

Thus, I have come from this way and unto Americus and then to the fleet, and to say I am Commander of the Fleet means from Americus, and then we are a part of the huge Ashtar Command. These are many fleets combined. Our fleet consists of about twenty seven great ships with all of the shuttles that apply to that theory or way of living. I am also known to many as husband of Hannona, or partner more in my way of speaking, being not into husband and wife in my way of speaking, but rather consummate life long partner—mate.

Hannona is the Commander of the ship that I am on now. She is also the Communications Officer for the fleet. I tell you this so that you know clearly of the status expected of both male and female upon Americus. There is no differentiation. At a time in the future, it is known, a female will be commander of the fleet, as it is chosen upon my planet that these roles alternate between the sexes as you call it on your planet. So last was a female and now it is I, Hatonn, and then it shall be again, a female. It is a rotation plan.

As I have come from a very long way to speak to you now, I cannot tell you all the things you desire to know, but some. First, I choose to acquaint you with how I am because I am broad in scope and in thinking. I apply these theories in my daily life. Do not be so abundantly concerned with the scientific application as to the fact that we exist in the same sphere or round and that in the thinking we become one, then I can give to you the application or the theoretical approach to the science. Always, it is vowed in the Light. Do not ever forget this, for the time is coming when you will command the ships again. What you give on Earth must be in the finest application.

As the ship, Molanya, is housing to five thousand people, it is approximately the size of a city and we call it a star city. Molanya is anchored beyond your sun. She is not expected to stay there forever. She is moving closer in the near future, we perceive. This is accorded through Ashtar Command. How it is positioning ships is up to the Great Council.

As of now, Molanya is beyond your sun in a location you could not perceive with your eyes or even a telescope. This is partially due to a magnetic shield which is deployed so as not to allow others to see. As you perceive it, however, in your memory bank, you will know Molanya. You have served up on her and as you think of the ways of the ships, you will begin to see glimpses of what the ship looks like.

Molanya is a great, great disc. You would call it silver, but it is more luminous than this, and luminous is to do with the incandescent materialization of the vibrations. Incandescent is a term applied to your light bulbs, I know this. This helps you understand that this great ship glows. Then you have it to be like a great disc. At the top of this disc is what we can call the control room. It is in your term round with windows and the panels that maneuver the ship and also maneuver the systems of the city. Below this, you have a great, great large area in the midst of this which is the huge ampitheater and this is for many things. The primary role here is that we view the Light.

This is something very different than you have experienced on Earth. It is when the Light manifests in actualization, when the Light becomes in the middle of the room, that we may sit in the great Source ray. The Source is God, and the Light that is given is the pure Light coming into the midst of this great ampitheater and allowing each individual to partake of its vibrational nature. This is similar to what you might say going to church.

It is not talking, it is not giving away anything. It is being with the Great Source Ray.

Other things are done in the ampitheater, to say we teach. We give each other lessons no one being the primary teacher. We give each other laughter as in you calling entertainment, and dance. And we receive visitors and at the time that you would come upon the ship, we would receive you in this great ampitheater. From this, you can go up and to the very perimeter of the ship, the very edge of this level and this is called the concourse, and this runs about the entire perimeter of the ship and there are windows and you can look out upon space. These are not windows like you know. This is a different material, so solid as to withstand any of the outside or inside pressures, but allowing ones to look beyond into the stars and suns that come and go in our vision.

As physical restoration is part of our practice, we do what you call running on this concourse. It is quite invigorating. As we have no systems of our home planet, but have had to manufacture them, we try to incorporate all the energies that we are, and we are physical people as you are. As you must run to stay whole, so we must, also. Although we are built different, it is similar. Then, if you can perceive that in this layer, there are other offices, so to speak.

The communications center is one of these. This is where Honnana has her patterns, her work, her living aspects. She is one of the most qualified individuals in the fleet and knows how to transfer the energy of communication from one series to another. This means that when a starship comes that cannot speak the languages of Earth and has not the communication frequency to connect, Honnana can bring through her voice, through her panels, this frequency, reduce it or amplify it, allow it to reconstruct so that those on Earth can hear. She is responsible for a great deal of the communication that comes through to this form so that it may be applied upon Earth. In this same area, there are other spaces that are utilized for other things, but you can envision that this is a working area as well as a restoration area.

Go down one level and you will perceive a town, very similar to what you would call a coastal town built upon cliffs with many apartments and beautiful exteriors. Allow to be in sequences down steps and having literal walkways and parks and an indoor sun as in your perception might exist. It is not literally a sun, but a source of energy of our spectrum that will not allow us to dwindle away. When you live on a starship, you must be prepared to live there many, many eons of time.

So, it is of a mode to calculate appropriately and plan for diversity, not one or two of us for any length of time. Sometimes, we come away for a day or two to another ship. Very, very rarely do we go back to our homeland. It is a very long journey and sometimes arduous depending upon the storms.

So, now we stay here about as the days of Earth come closer to the healing. Once or twice we allowed ourselves to go upon long journeys and so much happened while we were gone, we devoted our time now to stay. We decided not to leave and when one leaves now, it is usually to return and perhaps to retire from the service of the fleets. I tell you though it gets into your veins so that it becomes an extension of your planet and you do not desire so much to return to the planet. Some do not desire to even the fleets. They want to be upon the planet and that is their way to tend the accord of the planet.

As you observe the town itself, then you see within the parks there are fluids similar to water, not the same composition, crystalline in quality, lighter in substance, and there are birds there, in your terms, living creatures that inhabit our town. This is very much what you call a town.

Then below that, but not attached to, by another entrance you come to the place where the power for the ship radiates and you have first an area at the very bottom of the ship that is called the power center. This has a Commander, Tananya is her name. She is a Captain and she has the full ability to know exactly what to do to propel the ship and to make it stationery, to move it slightly right or left, to balance, to propel power to internal systems so that those aboard can live as they should and need to. The core of this energy you can call a dynamo although it does not move. It is the great crystals and this I wish to tell you. This is how the ship moves, sits, exists . . . the crystals.

In the center, at the very, very bottom of the ship in a dome shaped area that comes up into the ship, the ship is thus. Into the interior of the crystals are in their own component of housing. It is not black and dreary. It is light and when you go into this, you are bathed in the light of the crystals and energized by their Beingness. The center, the great crystal is the great power source and to each side, four more and then four smaller so that you have a synchronization and a literal magnification of the great center crystal depending on what needs to be done, and also directional maneuvering sending the energy into the ship for application or thrust to the outside.

In the power center where the panels are, you would see there also an abundance of living plants which would surprise you. You would think this to be scientific. It is living. It is being, therefore, you do not subtract any of the nature of it. You see this and also fluid called water running in what you call fountains. We call not these things the same. It is not the same vocabulary. There is another way we speak. I tell you things that may make a scene to you that you see it with your mind.

Tananya is tall and slim and very, very capable. She has been the Captain of this center for the last 3,000 years. This is timelessness in space. She is abundantly clear of her work and yet so light of heart as to be a child. This is what you would perceive if you come upon the ships, none of the dreary authority that you might associate with some human being adults—freedom to be in the joy of the child-like state. This is not childish, child-like, light and laughter.

Now, just beyond the periphery called the power center at the bottom of the ship there are bays and these are where the shuttles come and go. There are approximately ten, and they open as to slide up and down, and when the shuttle chooses to go, obviously, the door opens and when it comes back, it again opens and then it closes, and of course, you have here space atmosphere, so you never step out until you have been assured that the area has become appropriately balanced so you can breathe.

Then you have another sliding door that goes into the inner, a peripheral concourse which is not the huge concourse I spoke of. It runs all around the ship where the bays are. It has some other maintenance facilities attached.

As you move from the shuttle into the bay, then into the concourse, the door shuts, much as you have seen on the program called Startrek.

Let your mind use this information. It is given purposely. Startrek, it is a coding message for you. Pick up on it and use it. As you move into that concourse, then there is a place where you can become upwards and into the part of the ship that I have described, the upper concourse. There are also other ways. You don't have to go upon a transport. You can walk. It is encouraged.

As the ship herself housing approximately 5,000 people needs to be large, it is eight miles across. It does not move around much. When it moved to where it is, it was some 25 years ago. We had studied Earth population from this distance for this time. Also, some have come in shuttles closer, but this is not a system that we practice. There are others that do this. Our shuttles tend to get too hot in the atmosphere of the Earth. We have not converted our systems to allow us to come close without burning the shields and the skin. Obviously, this is not desirable. We don't do that.

As time progresses, we may move into more advanced units that we may also visit the surface, but it is not done on whim. It is all done on calculation and application of theory of Divine principles, therefore, a scientific is not what is to some of the people. A scientific mission is to determine how things are working in the region of Light manifestation or Light living, so to speak. It is coming from a different reasoning . . . soul's process.

Now, as you might endeavor to better understand the workings of the ships, do not demean or let go of any information that comes. Do not apply any theory that you think might be exact, but let everything come as general information. I counsel you this way, as you have already been accorded the exact task of accompanying the ships when that is right for you, then you don't have to learn anything. It is in your memory. As you view what is presented however it comes to you, view it with open understanding and you will remember. It will come again and again in flashes and in substance exactly stating to you, "Yes, I remember that, and there is a better way yet, I saw it when I was upon Uranus."

Then, when the time comes and your mind is completely open, you will have the memory track returned. You don't need it now. It would be confusing. You will have the full memory track and you will have Earth training. That's why you are here—to be trained in the ways of Earth that you can understand how people may need to change.

So, my sequence is concluded. I shall withdraw. I ask that you defer questions in the future to me. I can begin to answer you in your thought pattern. My name is called Hatonn and if you voice that, Hatonn of the starship, Molanya. Just call in your thoughts. Do not ask when you are busy. Ask when you have time to hear and the hearing process will begin, and you do know the way of bringing the Light down about you, is this not true? This is an absolute. It must be attended to. Do not for a moment imagine that what we do is of scientific nature. First, it is of Divine Intent and then scientific nature.

Now, I salute you, my friend. Yes, I shall see you again, not so long from now, but do not count the days.

(With the withdrawal of Hatonn, ones called the Group come forward.)

Greetings dear One. So, what did you think of that one?

"Interesting."

Yes, he is a great fan of the Light movement on Earth. He is very invested in it and that is clear that he respects you and your knowledge. Do not think that it is time to speak with your friends of these ways. Let them be investigating upon their own, for if they have an accord with the Light and the way that it moves, they will know so. For you see, you do not have to tell them anything until the time that they ask.

This is your personal journey. You have come a long way to be here, and it seems to start over but you are not starting over, this is just this segment, this lap, this leg of the journey, and the turning point is that the investment of energy that you have been given by Hatonn signals the respect and the fact that the Incorporated Legions wish to defer their appreciation to those who are on the ground.

You are one who is on ground who has served upon the ships, has been Commander of a ship for many times and it is wished that this be acknowledged. Therefore, Hatonn, being of high stature and courage and applicable Light, let us say, Hatonn is not stuffy, but we would wish you to know of his stature. As a Grand Master, you might think of this one. Therefore, we are very, very pleased for you.

Chapter 7

Kortron, Sananda, Cozann

May 9, 1988

There is telling me to "hurry up", but I wanted to tell you, when I came the other day, I couldn't spend much time, but I wanted to tell you that I am glad that you have come into the sensitivities. We have watched you for a long time. It is not appropriate to tell one thing to one that is coordinate when others are waiting. I have watched and I have waited. You are not diagrammatically superimposing to an Arcturian, you are factually remaining Arcturian.

"I have felt that, yes."

So, now that has come into its full expression. We can expect much attraction. We can expect much composure from each other and all the ones that come forward. There need not be any kind of turmoil between any of us even when we get distressed, we, as we pass through. I hope you understand this. When one comes or another and they are abrupt, it is because the wings of the eagles have not been clipped, they have been expanded. They have much to do.

"I have been trying, and I would like to prepare this place, or any space where I am, where you can come in and rest. I don't have to be here. It's a place where you can rest when you are in the area working with someone else. That's what I am trying to do in working with this room, etc."

It is done. There is one request—a little more green someplace.

"A little more green? Ok."

OK, that's about all. I just wanted to say that it was very, very convenient to stop by and that once I appealed to it, I asked you if it was appropriate, and you stated 'yes', and I came. I shall do so again. There will be many times. I am very grateful and I shall not stay a long time because it was important for the newcomers. They are not new in the energies, they are new in their awareness. I came once or twice before. It was not appropriate. I shall come and go swiftly and you will know it and think 'Hello, welcome' and we are gone. It is good to have stopping places because it gives us some rest.

Now, I go on my journey with some of my shipmates and some of your former ones are waiting. Everyone is impatient, you know that.

"I know that."

We are transmuting as much as we can as fast as we can. You are triggering the element of trust and a receptive mind. It takes a great deal of patience. The element of trust is the other side of suspicion. It is a very soft step. We are trying to allow it to become. We shall see. I am not skeptical of the possibilities. We are not counting the chickens . . .

"Do you expect great changes in California soon?"

I expect great changes in the bodies of the peoples. I do not know about the Earth coast. I think I will wait and see. It is not my domain. Anna is more involved. You may ask her.

"OK."

Since you have composed yourself, she will answer you, too. They are trying to transmute it to the bodies of the people. I think the wish is that the people would take more of the trauma thus allowing the timing to be simple.

"But does it help when they are not aware of what they are taking and they complain that they are taking it on? I mean that they are not actually knowing that they are transformers."

I think it will in the future. I think now they do not know, but wait until they have absorbed a few earthquakes. Wait until they have taken the tremors from the inner Earth and included that with their impact of daily living, then they will begin to understand. They may think it is a foreign power. That is the main thing they are aware of.

(Laughs) "The Russians . . . just kidding!"

(Chuckles) But also, space aliens. But the truth is there is nothing they can do. They cannot see us unless they trust. The second truth is I will set the purpose, I will deliver, I will come to any who call. I will not stand about and wait. Now, I must go.

"OK. Thank you, Kortron."

Be in good stead.

"Thank you."

I am Sananda.

"Hello Sananda."

Even Sananda needs a rest sometimes.

"Yes."

I appreciate this device of bringing in the Light. It allows us to enter and be casual.

"Yes."

To be present without being commanded.

"Yes."

Sometimes, I come into the frequency just to see what is happening. Sometimes, I correlate with another's energy to allow them to come into your presence. Sometimes, I am silent. Sometimes, in the essence of what is being wrought on the planet, I ask questions. I ask, "What is it about for you? How are you?"

"I am very fine tonight! I was having real difficulty with the energy last week and the week before. I couldn't get rid of . . . was blocked. It was like entirely rigid from my shoulders almost, well, from halfway up my head almost to my waist, but I have gotten it all worked out partly with Catherine's energy and then with being on the Coast and walking. I feel like I have cleaned the etheric today."

The wind does that.

"Yes. I feel really good, much more powerful than I have felt for a long time."

So going away from here for a time, going away and allowing the routines to be . . . there are many positive factors. I am glad.

Sometimes when I come to disciples, I seem to expect much. Some understand that and some don't. That is perceived by myself and I hold to the currents so they may understand. They don't expect me to be as unadulterated as I am. Some expect me to be sanguine. Some expect me not to request much nor to give orders. My command that is to serve. When one serves, one then requests. It is not orders that they receive. It is that I expect them to respond.

"Yes."

In Sananda, in the privacy of your understanding, you will perceive differences in my actions. It is because the time is now for this truth to be spoken and there is no other way than to step forward. When you were with the one called Jesus and the others, those who were there often saw this command. 'Come to the forefront'. It never expected another to be other than their utmost. It did expect that, and it was stated thus and so I shall be.

When a person is ready for my council, that is the beginning and they ask advice. When one is ready for discipleship, they don't ask advice, I tell. I become stronger and stronger and there is noticed that I move faster and faster. This is the way. Now, when you have council, there will be that which is your own to speak, for you shall not just ask, you will tell. Another must come into their way and thinking, and you have been rewarded many times. Allow this to travel back and forth between ones.

The people will come, the people will pass. Tell them so. Between your comrades, act. You have been . . . you know. If I surface to tell you some things, I shall be exactly as we are together as Commanders. I shall not expect undue respect, but also I shall not expect undue servitude. I shall expect that you command me as I you and I shall respond to that. So then we ask each other questions. You say, "What do you think?" I say, "What do you think?" We shall have full council. Others will come and be seated and you will know it, and as you are thinking, we will communicate back and forth. It will not be able to be recorded, but it could be noted upon the pad.

"Yes."

When a council setting is due, it will come to your notice. Sometimes with the accumulation of energy that you have allowed here, there will be some hundred seated, you know this. Sometimes, when you bring your students, fellow workers into this setting, they shall in their way bring to this setting, many multitudes.

"Yes."

As then it is assimilated, allow them to express what they are feeling and seeing because the council will be served in that manner. It will come forth. We will have practice sessions, literally we will create here the setting for council whereby each one will speak the voices of their peoples. They will need practice. Do your work to free them to that acceptance.

State to them, "I know that this is a setting for council. I know that we have been called here. We have several hours. Let us make tea. Let us speak. Let us be with this. Tell me if you would what you are feeling. Tell me what you are seeing and hearing if this is such. Tell me what the thoughts are and we will begin to understand. This is practice.

You are teacher, you know this, but not just of the novice. A teacher frees. On Earth it has been the democratic method of allowing the teacher to be in the mode of freedom only to the point of 'What kind of dictation shall we put forth?'

"Yes."

Truly, through the demeanor that you have is mutual respect, dignity granted, the way together that is Truth, thus, by perceiving that as Truth, allowing their modest contribution to be noted and respected, they become more within moments. Thus, you the Teacher, frees and they become the teachers. That is your desire. More than you have thought of before, they shall become Master Teachers. They know it, but they know not, more and more, tens of times, twenty. So, that is coming soon and I am their Voice. You can call me and I shall speak through you always when it is necessary.

Do not be modest. Know that you deserve/ desire this comraderie. Allow us to be in the simplest terms without biasness, without Beingness but with a great deal of gayety, and hopefully, not seriousness. The maneuver, or the exercise, the mission, or the endeavor is coming closer to fruition, I can tell you this. I will not tell you all of the rest. I will tell you that at conclusion . . . fruition. We have objectives. We see that the time is right for some changes. I will tell you more about these later.

"For instance, in one day last week there was the blowing up of the rocket fuel plant, the fire in the oil rig off shore, the fire in Los Angeles in the big bank building. They are all related, aren't they?"

Ummhummm.

"The one in Los Angeles was simply to show how unprepared the people are. It's very interesting to watch who ties them together and who doesn't."

(Chuckles) Sounds like a cosmic pyromaniac, doesn't it?

"I thought it was pretty humorous myself. (Laughs) I thought my friends had been very busy."

Yes. It is putting them into combustible vibration. It is allowing modes to be expressed without doing much harm.

"Ummhummm. Very little harm . . . amazing."

You will see these things again. In the midst of that, do not forget to have lots of fun. Arcturians are learning to have fun. Kortron is not an Arcturian, but he should be. Do you know who he is?

"I don't know where he comes from. He has been a teacher of mine, has he not?"

He is part of the Arcturian Brotherhood and he has motivated his clientele and cherished you. He is broad of chest, large of heart, strong and quick upon the Way, thoughtful, considerate, highly intelligent, a very skilled teacher. A teacher who frees and is modest.

So, you will learn much from these ones and they from you, and as your other friends come into their knowing, allow them their full accord. Soon you will be able to hear those ones speak. Soon you will have several friends who will have ones speak through them.

"That will be very, very fun. I have heard through a human in Seattle that you will appear on June 29th to those who meditate. Is that something you are planning?"

It is not in my mind to say so right now, but perhaps.

"But if we pray, maybe."

I can appear to you anytime. You know this. How foolish to state one day. I am always available.

"I know."

Now I go.

"Thank you so much."

Be of strong heart and safe journey. I cherish you always.

"Thank you so much."

I am Cozann.

"Hello Cozann."

I hope you notice how straight I sit.

"I do."

There seems to be nothing more distressing to those Arcturians who are out and about than to find a slumpy one.

(Joyce laughs)

She (the channel, Gayl) doesn't slump, but articulately we straighten the spines of many. You may find this when we are here. Isn't that interesting? I am an Arcturian, too.

"Wonderful. So glad to meet more and more and more."

I am out and about because I have been incorporating some energies into my system you might want to know about.

"Tell me."

When I came to this planet, I did not find an abundance of understanding. I didn't stay long. That was about 1978. I took back my energy system and I went out to do the work elsewhere. I didn't find the Arcturian delegation a place to do that substantially. I wanted to work with humans. I didn't want to work with humans in outer space. I wanted to work with humans in inner space.

I went about through the friends of conveyance, I went to the ships and I talked to the Commanders and I made the statement that I would choose to work in the spatial dimension. They suggested that I come into connection with one called Joyce Strahn. That was 1978 and we began then an interaction that you might not know much about, but maybe you do.

I came and I stayed and I watched and I learned and I gave instruction and sometimes you perceived it as disorder. Sometimes, we spake upon the airwaves at night. Sometimes, we sat peacefully and we kept information. And I stayed and I watched and I gained energy because I could stay about your air waves because you are Arcturian. I figured if you were here, I could stay here. I didn't have to come and go so much, but I didn't stay beyond 1982. Then I began to gather energy and I began to work with other people.

I came back. I am here. I am incorporating to get more energy. I like to work with humans. I think they are nice. I don't care if I am Arcturian and they are human. I don't care if they are human/human as you are Arcturian/Arcturian (laughs). Do you know why I have a sense of humor?

"Why?"

I want you to guess. I have been here since 1978. I have been with humans. That is why you will find that I have more of a sense of humor than some of my fellow Arcturians who are out.

"How did you breathe without all of the rose quartz?"

I had a time for awhile and I couldn't even say my name sometimes, I was so weak, but I decided to try it and I gained strength. The thing that gave me strength was empathy. There are vibrational tones that the Universe allows to be what you are, to choose and to discern, I know that. There are substances of energy that are available. I will stay and I want to teach you these things that will assist you—class transcriptions.

When one decides that one shall have empathy to love unconditionally, that is called compassion toward a species that is abundantly perceiving itself as rude, aggressive, destructive, happy . . . all these things. When one decides that one shall have compassion, one begins to be of a substance of vibration that allows one to stretch further. In other words, when one makes one decision of that nature from the higher accords, one eliminates the need to assess and make decisions upon multiple other possibilities. One becomes.

Now in my thinking, I am one of the strongest teachers on the planet because I know this. I am strong for the humans. I am strong for those who have come cross from other lands. I know this thing surely that human beings ought to be taught this mode, this way they are to know that by essence of their viability, they become able to survive in many conditions. I don't think that this will be necessary for a time. I think it might become necessary.

I know that when I came I was rash. I know not what my delegation perceived, but they do not condemn. We choose. We are our own Commanders. I chose not to be associated with a quadrille or a group setting, I chose to be individual. In that essence, I have gone very strong, not only etherically, but physically in my form as I am. My spirit is stronger, my self is stronger. I am able to be where others cannot. You can send me to the inner city. I can survive.

When I became to this place, I decided I would work with humans on their level, one on one and I nearly died, in your terms. I became unto their way. I knew them, I trust them, I understand them. They do not know me. It does not matter to me. That is my advantage. I am grown from before I came.

"Are you working only with Arcturian people?"

I am working with the Arcturian delegation at this point to teach them those things that they dare not not know.

"That's right."

They becoming what they are and knowing what they are allow me that stead even before they guess what I might present. That is how our peoples are and others from far lands. They know each other. They trust. You do not have to prove yourself. Yes, I am teaching them of these findings. I am a scientific philosopher. I perceive that human beings know a lot of things that they have not let out because they have fear of being discovered.

"Yes."

I perceive also that human beings have a gauntness about them. In their seeking, they are starving. They are becoming into a time when they must have answers.

"Yes."

In this, they are granted great understanding from myself, and I know that there are humans who seem not to be anything of value and they act that way. I see this, but I know that beneath that there lies a valiance. I know this. So let us not pretend that human beings cannot do things that are destructive, not be vandals, not be trifling with others feelings. Let us be truthful and state, "Yes, indeed, human beings have these traits, also that of their highest magnificence."

"Yes, I know."

What they know is that in their truth, they lie about themselves and they cannot accept that which they really are.

"Ummmhumm"

As you know, the magnificence of royalty and the magnificence of traditional religion have made it almost impossible for them to understand what they truly are. They have given away their power far before they were born.

"Right."

These ones on this Earth now do not have any idea how to retain their sovereignty.

So, I have dwelt among them and I perceive that I can teach them. I perceive that I can teach those of you who have come about into your high space and I can teach you to teach others.

"Good."

And I can teach the delegation and all of the others who wait. They have not assumed that human beings are wrong or all bad. They just do not know how great recovery power can be. Human beings need to concentrate on two elements : 1) is sovereignty; 2) is the actualization process of rising on the energy.

When you state that you love someone, it is really very difficult. Inside, it doesn't work. You can state, I am becoming love because I choose to. It has nothing to do with another person and you can state, I do not have to love another person until the time is right, and it shall be right. This is something you could use as a text. I could give it to you.

Becoming love is an excellent process. Commander Sananda has a vibration. It always "is". He is as close to God as any shall ever know. There are others of his capacity, but let us use this one. He is as close to God as any shall ever know. By maintaining that reverence in a Light vibration, one becomes as Sananda is.

"I am very willing, you know. I would be so willing if you want to write through me . . . whatever. There needs to be, I find it . . . I have analyzed this thing with the classes every way I know and I know that analysis is not the answer. The answer is what feels right. I do not see that the classes were devised out of ego. At the time that I wrote those, I was at the bottom of my emotional pit. It was out of what I know . . . this is what I am taught.

It was out of gratitude for that learning. I sometimes wonder . . . are they too powerful . . . are they too strong, but then if I dilute them, it weakens it. I don't feel we have all the time in the world. We don't have till next semester, you know.

So then I say, why do they drop out? But what I believe is that the ones I am teaching are the ones trained by the hierarchy and that the ones who drop out are the ones not ready for the commitment, but it bothers me then to know, why are there only two when there should be two hundred? What can we do to make them understand?"

First of all, the way on this series of lessons qualifies you as a Master Teacher for the human form. Allow that to be. Tis done. You will find that the weeding out process is not a matter of your popularity, it is the wisdom of the Light agents who state to these ones, "It is not your time. You are not ready to get this," because you need to have those who can take the fastest and the most.

When you have this criteria set up, it is not to your sense fulfilling, perhaps, and it is frustrating to have them drop out, and perhaps even to the essence that you would like to teach full time. But I cannot tell you to teach full time yet . . . not yet. This advanced work that you are doing now is cause for you to understand how it will be. Everything is being placed in position. It is training for you as well as them.

When, then you put these motivations into effect and you see a class fill up and gradually dwindle, it is because you need those specific few more than you need the many. They learned enough. They are well on their way. Release them to their growth of weakness.

So, then let us say that you have improvised a set of teachings that can be given to the youngest and smallest and they can abide with it, and if they can't, then they don't need to be there. There are other teachers. And if they cannot stay the duration, they need not be here. You need those ones who stay because then you will shoot the energy faster. Give them as much as you have devised and more, faster and faster. That is when we will come. You must do as fast as possible all that you can.

That is why you are having a great deal of health interference. You are being given manifestations to allow you to do this work as it is. It is important to support the field of energy for the teaching. We are supporting the work as it exists. It is much better for us to support and encourage the existing systems than to create another source of income. It is much better for us to support sales of houses and land because that is a motion. People need those spaces. They must be able to move freely. It is much better than trying to improvise another source of income.

When you have such an action as several hundred, that would be a class action, that is the populace. That is not the time. You want the Master Teachers to come forward and they will and you will know it. They are worth twenty to one. So then, they come forward at the moment that the classes reached its ongoing size . . . it may start with twenty, dwindle to ten. You may end up with six. That's your number and you know it.

Then you tell them, "OK, that's my signal to start the activation of energy and allow you to rise very quickly and we will begin to do things in addition. They need to know the substance of the text and then allow them to know that we believe they are complete. They can come back for some other things, but they are complete. That is where I come in. That is where the substance of Korton is and Zeron is. That is where it will allow them to feel comfortable with the merger of energy with their unit chief. That is a big job. You do not need to have numbers of people to do that. That is a very big job.

If you were trying to accomplish that with the original twenty, they would be very frightened. They would cry out and you know those are signs of witchcraft and anything that frightens you. One is to protect your substance and allow you to focus in upon those who are the strongest. It is not that we are picking some out so that others are favored.

"I know."

It is to allow the strongest to come forth. They are known by their vibration. Everything is done this way. When one sees that vibrationally, it cannot compute, they remove themselves. We can give them credit, they know that. That is a high and advanced subject.

"I find it quite humorous that when it comes to the part of the classes where they have to find out what is holding them back and what is limiting them, they don't show up. I can almost know who isn't going to be there the weeks that we really have to work, because they are happy to pick up all of these little things, but when it comes to digging in and really making tracks as to what we have to do in order to go on, it is not comfortable."

Ummm humm. You might want to devise in the future, a simpler set of tracks and let them go that far because this set of tracks will impose itself at some point in their life. They are going to have to do that anyway. You are offering to expedite. If they choose that not, they come in another way.

You might find that you want two sets of tracks. I don't mind either way. I don't care. I am only interested in the ultimate outcome of perceiving that which actuality is Truth, is Divine Statement and I am not even in accord to state that I like them. I don't. I don't like all the humans, I don't like all the Arcturians, I don't like all Venusians, but I love them all. That is the need in the highest sense of loving, of letting go whatever they are performing, and the amusement that I feel is not that I have gained this great manner of speaking humor. The amusement is in the observation.

Some would state that I was to seat myself back and observe and laugh at them. No, I am laughing at their antics and I am thinking sometimes, you silly humans, don't you know what you are doing? And now you are truly very funny to me, but at another time, it's not funny.

So, the humor of Arcturians is going to rise dramatically once they drop themselves down to the humanness of the moment. If they want humor, they are not going to be able to stand back and watch other people who have laughter as a trait and absorb it, they are going to have to get in there with their shoes off. Tell them that when they come around. Tell them I said so. They don't need . . . .

I am a former Commander. Do you know how it is when in your land one is in the military and they suddenly resign and begin to talk peace?

"Umm humm."

Well, here is a former Arcturian Commander saying, "Take off your shoes, get your feet in the mud, and learn how to laugh. So . . .

"Is it better to try to maintain in the city so people could come easier for classes, or would it be better to try to somehow get a piece of land that had the trees and the water . . . I am feeling so strongly that I should get out of the vibrations of the city, but I know that that entails the money for the upkeep as well as the land, the fencing, the heavy work that in this human female form is hard for me to do. It also would be a lot of energy to maintain the place, plus try to maintain the money through the real estate, plus try to do the classes. What do you feel is best for me?"

I think that it will come of its own time and you won't have to do it. I think that more than that, more than that energy and time and money, you should take more time off, because we will bring to you quality listings. We think that you should take time just to walk by the pond here where it is, to go to the big pond on days, to go to the falls and immerse yourself more.

Stay where you are at this time knowing that will come. You see it is just in the action and you see it. That is what you feel. It is in the future and you see it but you don't have to do anything about it. I think it is better to take more time and service yourself then to make that kind of change, because you will lose a great deal that you have gained. And it will come.

"I feel so much better at the coast. My energy is so much better there. Not to live there . . . I don't mean that, but to go there more often."

That's what I think—go there every other week. Get your friends to go and share a place. If you could manage every week, do that. Do truly take time to walk in the morning. You cannot survive if you don't have that kind of activity. You need something to dance.

"I know."

Loosen up your Arcturian heritage. Goodness sakes! Loosen up the form. Just laugh. If there is anything silly . . . that is what Arcturians seem to negate in their process. They are getting there. Kortron is one of the better ones. He is not Arcturian full blood—he's a half breed. (Laughs)

"I felt such emotion when he came in. It just really welled up in me. Such a recognition, but of course, I don't know where from, but I really like him."

He is your parent from another time and teacher. He's a former teacher and a former parent. How do you like that across lives? There he is all at once. Many things there, but primarily what you feel is the magnetism of the personage. It's mostly what it is. He's a very powerful leader and healer. He brings people together. By his presence, he brings people forward. He once served much as Sananda does now. He comes from the same position, and he brought forward to many peoples from planetary systems that which Sananda does here. He is here serving as an Arcturian Commander. That tells you the magnitude of this effort.

"Amazing!"

Yes, it is an all out effort. So, the good of the people depends on the good of ones like you. The good of ones like you then depends on the good of ones like us and on and on. Primarily your interest is preserving your body form. The rest is taken care of. You need not ever write another lesson plan. It is done at the instant. You can incorporate wisdoms into your teachings at the moment they will come through.

I highly recommend that you do less for the students and more for yourself, less for the real estate and more for yourself. It is all coming. If you want to take yoga classes, or I suggest just dance—music. I like hearing music. Have you ever heard Arcturian music?

"No." (Laughs) "What is it like . . . like the Gregorian chants or something?

(Laughs) Don't you think that's silly? Fine, I think that is funny. Arcturians are funny. Wagner—Arcturians love Wagner.

"Boom, boom, boom."

We like Greta Garbo, too, but that's rather serious.

"Are Aleckatron and Rozann still here?"

Umm humm.

"I wish I could get . . . I can't . . . all I get is a little bit of writing from them. I don't know how to bring them in."

What do they say?

"Just simply that they want to make greater contact and that we need to get a signal device and nothing more. I can't bring in anything more. I have no trouble with Zeron. Zeron I can feel . . ."

Yes, that's because of who he is. Let's see. They are coming. They said Gregorian chants is exactly appropriate.

(Laughs.)

They are not sulking. They say that you have been able to receive them. It is just that there is a motivation device in the cellular structure that comes from the time setting of your birth. Motivation meaning not your willingness psychologically, it is timing that states that it is important to hear those who are of your birth nature. Do you understand that?

"I hope so. I think maybe that I do."

All right. The brain cells that are not activated . . .

"Yes?"

A timing device, but what it is is an opening process, a setting that will allow you to hear more articulately those of your nature. The time for the device has not been composed yet. They have not decided when to open this setting. They want to hear more from you on your right for this. How do you choose with the many to be articulate? How much do you want to be speaking? You see, you have transposed quite a bit. What they are saying is be careful. Let's be careful not to overdo it.

"Oh, I am trained to speak in front of people, you know. I don't mind that at all. I also feel that I could write books with your help, you know. This has always been in my mind. I would love to do that sort of thing."

Rozann wants to try that. That would be a good escape valve to experiment and just to allow the energies to play.

"Allow him to do the typing?"

Well, first you will see some stretching exercise. He is not used to this.

It is an action he has not tried.

"I tried that one time, but I just won't sit there for hours."

Oh, no, you don't want to do that. But also, the timing must be open or it can't occur. I must ask them about this—the Arcturian bunch.

"Are they all male? I don't know any of them that are female."

Rozonn is almost. Androgyny is very prevalent on your planet and that does not correlate anything with Earth codes at all.

OK. You have got one named Coton here now. He says it is time for the device. They can arrange it for this night time.

"I would like it to get going. Enough of this."

All right. They are saying "Don't be aware that the timing device is an imposition or a negation or a time bomb going off. They are saying it will seem a little peculiar, but they are fixing it. It will be almost like a burning sensation in the left ear. It will come in through spatial dimension, then to the cellular structure with very long thin . . . so small. He says that is why a lot of people who are taken to the ships don't understand that they are programmed and adjusted to open and they become very frightened. It will seem to be a burning sensation, but it will be at the very most two or three minutes. Don't allow any modification of the schedule set allowed

110

to be stated to you in voice and thought. You will know. They will tell you what to do in the sleeping room.

"That's where the strongest rose quartz is, though I've worked on it a lot out here, also. They like it out here. They like the big couch in there." (Laughs)

There is a whole bunch. They are having a conference. Rozann says, "OK, I've got to go now. See you later. I am coming in style." Let's call him she because really he is she. He is very tranquil energy. Aleckatron says, "Don't be frightened by the imposition of wills upon your outstretched hand. It will be OK."

Just make it available so that it is there and then they decide. Then they can say, "I know about that."

I went to some movies.

"Oh, you did."

I found some humans who know about these things and they would allow me to look. They didn't need to know that I was Arcturian. They didn't have fear and I didn't frighten them so I got to see some movies. Do you know the story about Goldilocks?

"Yes."

That's a strange one, isn't it?

"Yes. In the children's stories here, the animals eat up the people or the big bad wolf, and they are afraid. They are very bad. We could use much improvement in the writings for children."

Something else that I noticed is that in San Francisco there is a lot of boring escapades on the screen and on the stage. I don't understand that. I see also a lack of enthusiasm in the energy system of the people in the inner cities. I think the premise for their existence is outer external sensory application.

"Yes."

So I see not much vitality and enthusiasm. Don't you think that is true?

"Yes, they are dead inside. It is apathy."

They are looking for something from out here to stimulate their life. You are exactly right.

"Exactly, but it begins with their God. They put their God out there somewhere and that way they don't have to take any responsibility. They just feed off things that will give them pleasure, but they don't need to take responsibility because they can go to church and say, 'God will take care of it and I don't have to'—see. I've never understood that since I was a child on Earth. I've never understood that concept."

Now I see them desperately looking for something that they can use.

"Because none of this sensory stuff fills them up. It only gives them pleasure for the moment. It does not feed them intellectually, emotionally, or any other way."

Do you know that that is one of the reasons for the incestual violence on the planet?

"Oh, that is getting to be something else, isn't it? It's because it is taboo to do this kind of activity with someone else, so in the confines of the home no one should know. The abuse of people is really . . ."

That's why I think we should remove some people soon, but that's not my choice. I don't get to make that decision. I'm going back to the council gathering for two or three times in the days ahead, but I should be back sometime next week.

"Good. That will be wonderful."

And we shall come into some kind of substance together. I am trying to set up patterns where I can communicate freely with those in various parts of the country so as to balance out the energy.

"I think it is wonderful that you have been able to live in the energy since 1978."

I think it is wonderful that I survived to tell you about it!

"There weren't many Lightworkers working very hard then in 1978."

Well, now I can move about and I don't have to create the environment. I am stronger but it is because I have adapted to Earth. That can happen. It happens when one decides to become physically fit. They think they are tearing themselves down, but they are not. If I were to become a being on Earth, which I might someday, I would keep myself fit.

Well, this is charming and I could stay a long time, but I think I should go. I love this space to sit there in that chair.

"That's where I do my meditating. The chair seems to be alive."

Mmmm hmmm.

"There's a lot of clutter in here now. We've had so many people, but it is usually more in order than it is right now."

Yes, an Arcturian would say that.

"I do believe cleanliness is next to Godliness. (Laughs) I can't stand a mess. This will have to be all cleaned before I go to bed tonight."

And orderliness comes between cleanliness and godliness.

Ummm hmm. Well, I've got to go. I've got to be busy. I think I need a vacation.

"I think so, too. Why don't you take a little extra time. Where do you go for the council meeting? Is it on a ship or another planet?"

It's on a place called Totham which is . . . it's kind of like a ship, but it isn't. It's more like a floating slab of rock and it has a great temple. There's a painting in her mind by Gilbert Williams . . .

"Yes, I was just thinking the same thing."

It's a creation and it was designed particularly for these things because it is delightful.

"Ummm humm."

Many people enjoy going there. It is not just a one-time experience. One in trance form desires to go back. You are fed . . . nurtured.

"If you see my last Father, Eldon, on the way somewhere, say Hello."

He shall be there. He is part of the Council. Ok, I am going. I shall tell him "Hello" and all the others.

"Tell him I am doing much better—growing, lots more."

I will, I surely will and when I fly over on the way to the Coast after the Council meeting, I will send you a beam.

"OK."

And I will be back a couple of days later.

"Thank you so much."

Chapter 8

Ashtar and the Kids

June 19, 1989

Gayle did this channeling for three high school students who were part of a group of high school students that I had worked with over an eighteen month period of time. They were awesome . . . and working with them was one of the highlights of my teaching the Divine Mysteries in this lifetime.

I welcome you. I am Commander Ashtar.

Do you know of me?

"Yes."

So that I may begin without explaining myself. I am very glad to see you.

"Thank you for coming here."

It is my privilege. How I am here is telepathic in your thoughts, but if I say to you, telepathic is but a description and that I am more here than you might guess, I can say it is molecular extension. Do you understand this term? A portion of me comes through time and space to you to inhabit this form for a moment and to be with what is humanism.

For this factual event which is in the 3rd dimension of your planet, there is that which is necessary for me to inhabit and that is a form for now. Soon you will be able to hear me, and perhaps, sense/see me without this action. That is what I desire.

If I say to you that you are inhabited by Spirit of your own Self, you understand that clearly and if I say that the Spirit of this body has chosen to step aside and that I now inhabit this body, you understand that. If I said then, perchance one or two of you is located, also, far above upon a ship in the interior, can you understand that? You can be in two places, in fact, more. We shall discuss what is most necessary. There is much to know.

There is much to tell, but all of it that I might say and you might ask, you already have. It is just waiting. This service we perform together is for a moment in your time and less than a moment in my time because mine is not linear time. If I can but enhance your awareness of who we are, I shall have done my work because you will be able to pick up the threads and follow unto that which is the vastness and know what you really came to do.

My work is with the fleets, as they are known, but these fleets are not like anything that you have ever seen. These vessels of Light illumine beaming Light into the night of this time upon Earth. These vessels are whence you came. You were there. You are there. Also you are Spirit of Earth. Does this confuse you at all? If you have confusion, please tell me.

I do not know, at your age, what you have learned about what we are, except that you have been in the fond regard of this Being who knows all, so I assume that you are well trained. I desire neither to inhibit another's growth with too much information or to withhold information, so you must be ready to ask the things you wish to know.

If a ship projected a beam of, how shall we say, acquirement or knowledge into you upon this surface, you would be able to readily hear and feel, see and know what is on shipboard. A Being that is able to come from a very small monosyllabook, this is in your language meaning less than words to you, but in the concepts of your reality, your vocabulary—that Being and there are many coming to you constantly, being available to you, feeding you, telling you things—that's one of the reasons that you have ended up here.

You are guided, not as puppets, never accept this, because you are cared for a great deal. You are asked to be present here so that we may actually speak about these things. The beams are the ways of knowing where you are, what is your interest, and how it is going, and to hear your questions and to help you find the answers.

If you know the beam exists, you can ask directly into your home station. This is ground, this is ground crew, this is the surface, but above in the skies, there are many vessels and they await the awareness of the humans that they shall work with. If you have seen drawings, pictures, photographs of these possibilities, then you are not limited in what we may talk about. How I wish you to proceed this is that you could look into the interior of these vessels and see that which you really are. If one says to me, I am not interested in the ships, I say, "Fine. It does not matter." I do not care what one chooses, that is their business. If they are interested, I am available.

I have a large scope in my work. I am the one who is responsible to coordinate all of the fleets, all of the ships from all of the galaxies. I have come forth. Why they have come forth, I think you know. It is to supplement that which is the energy field upon this plane. If one looks at the declining environment, that is reason enough to think that somebody might come and help. If one looks then at society and its confusion, that is another reason. If one looks at the broad scale of fact of what the turmoil has done to personages called human, it is another reason.

Many humans are frightened, very much afraid to know themselves, let alone I, hummm, and let alone the ship. If one then understands that this is the time of grace coming upon this plane, and that is what we are really talking about, we are not really talking about space ships. We are really about the grace, the Oneness that we all share.

So, my work is the same is yours. It is just that you are here and I am elsewhere. You are teacher and you know it. You are computer expert and you shall translate the languages that come from afar for human beings to understand. You have a way with these machines (talking to the second boy), also, and how you will enact them is far from your memory at this time. You did design what you would do here. Do you have any concept of what it was?

Do you know that before you come in a body you choose the things that you shall be? Let us say it is on a grand scale. I shall not be able to explain it because that is for you to discover. It has to do with mathematics. It has not to do with Earth mathematics. I do not know if you favor mathematics, but if you do not, do not worry because they are not the same. They are primary and they really don't improve the capacity to understand what you shall bring forth.

If a mathematician told you how to design the skin of a spaceship, you might be surprised because you know there is more to it than that, and there is more to it than that of a metallurgist with the knowledge of what certain stresses can withstand. And if the geographer said, "This is the terrain," you would also know that. Let us say you are many layered, my friend, and the concepts you shall bring through shall be assists to those who truly wish to know who we are.

If you like to be with those of the Devic Kingdom (talking to the girl), I can only suggest that you have come from the Stars and you know well how to understand the language. As you came upon the beam upon the ship, I watched. Do you know how one might come upon the beam into the infant form of a human?

All right, inside each ship there is a transport beam. Do you watch Startrek?

TD—"Definitely, yes."

This is very much accurate. There are some things of the program that are not, but very much, very close to what the actuality is. As you are aware that it is time to become in form on this planet, a Being such as yourself presents themselves. This is after much training. It is not a surprise appointment. This is an awareness and a great dedication, and as a ship comes close and the time is right and the infant form is available, chosen, coordinated, etc because you chose your parents, you step into this dematerialization beam. You understand what that is, don't you?

TD—"Umm hummm."

Think about how they step into the beam on the program and they turn into Light. Dematerialization—and those molecules can be sent in that suspended state through time and distance to rematerialize. Now, if I told you if you were actually not a Spirit in the body but a form within a body, would you be surprised?

TD—"It would be very interesting."

So, it would mean you are different from some humans, but there are others like you. It would mean that you have a vibrational rate that is above the Earth plane dimension and you inhabit this form as an existent total Being much as one might stand here of your Nature Kingdom and speak to you through this form. You live within this human facility.

TD—"I am not quite sure what you meant when you said a form within a form. For some reason that is not clear to me."

You had a molecular structure . . .

TD—"Right."

You are not a Spirit Being. You had a condensed molecular structure. (To Joyce) Do you have anything of fairies about in photographs so she could see?

Joyce—"Yes."

The fourth dimension has a vibrational rate above that of the third dimension awareness, so your eyes sometimes can pick up Lights, colors.

Joyce—"Like this or like this."

Yes, this is a good example.

A Being that you might not see has been painted for you to see. Now, as to the wings, let us say that you do not have these wings, but similar character. This form, this vibration is just beyond your sight. It vibrates at a faster rate. It vibrates at a faster frequency than yourselves here. That form that you are lives compatibly within this form just as though it were a Spirit and you were here invigorating the flesh. Understand?

Joyce—"Is she from the Nature Kingdom on Earth or is she from another planet?"

She is from another planet.

Joyce—"But she is equivalent to—she is a deva in a human form."

Yes. Do you understand this?

TD—"I think I do, but does that mean that I have a Spirit somewhere, or . . . and that's what I am getting a little bit confused about."

Ahhh. Now we must expand this. Let us talk about the cosmic cellular structure. Let us just describe what you really look like and she and she and this form, also, and I because everything is One. You know that. You have heard that said, but how can that be? We wonder sometimes.

Here is your form. Going out from it, there is Spirit essence. Beyond that, a rate or a sphere that is your Celestial Being. That is you, you, you. Everyone is created this way. Beyond that, to the ends of eternity, to include all of the Universes, all of the dimensions, is your cosmic Beingness. Now, it has this form, this Spirit essence, your Celestial Beingness and that is too large to imagine. It is not contained within this room.

(Laughs)

And keep going beyond your form and it is your Cosmic Beingness. That is the Oneness. That is where everyone is one. You see, we cannot not be One. We are. It is the structure. And so each cell in this form is also designed this way. In all of that, you have had Spirits. You, yourself, designed Spirits to be upon other planes, but at this point in time, you have become one of the Devic Kingdom and you still are. You brought the full impact, in other words. You did not leave the form behind.

So, if we wanted to say strategically to ease your mind that you are a Spirit within form within form.

TD—"OK. That makes me feel better." (Laughs)

It does not mean that you do not have a Spirit, it means that you have designed this to the best advantage for this plane, this planet.

Joyce—"She is a high powered deva."

She is.

Joyce—"She is a purple deva. She is a queen."

Yes. Yes.

Joyce—"I knew that."

This would be a very close photo to telling you more about what you really are. In the sense that you function very well in form, it is not a detriment to know that you have this awareness this way, but to some it is very hard here when they are of the devic nature. They are very gentle and fragile and they become fearful upon this plane. When they have friends who are so shy, they cannot come out, delicate creatures. You may know people your age and might associate with them who are so very shy. It is a terrible ordeal to be a teenager in that state.

Joyce—"Why would she choose to take on human form?"

Because it is necessary for the re-creation.

Joyce—"And her purpose then is to bring forth to the masses that there are devas. Is she to write and draw and teach about devas?"

It is to draw, it is to tell, not so much to write. You will find this coming around in time.

TD—"Interesting, because just now, I mean, I feel that I, myself, was feeling very shy at times and now things are slightly changing and I am talking more and I'm speaking more and able to communicate more, so that's very interesting."

You have learned several languages, have you not?

TD—"Ummm . . ."

It is easier to speak to the peoples of the nationality, if you speak their words. You will find many of the artists of this nature depicting that which you are and you will find the artists depicting that which you aren't.

If we said then that each of you came here via a ship, that is not exaggeration. Many, many came via this method because they needed to be here so completely, so totally. However, two of you have transferable forms (the two boys). You do not, you are here (speaking to TD). You are there and here. (speaking to TM) Do you have any questions about how this works?

Joyce—"What does he do upon the ship? What is his job on the ship?"

Well, to use language terms and third dimensional terms, computer programming, but that is not sufficient to tell you what he does. Coding devices—this would help you learn a little bit about what is coming. When the energy systems of this awakening society lift up and begin to be more whole and available, society will be free, and they will seek to know what they really are. Simply put, they are God manifest, but they don't know that and the ones that have tried to find out have been stifled at every turn. So, from every vantage point, from every moment, every possibility, we feed those who are awakening. It doesn't matter to me how one looks higher, just, I ask that they look, but when they have looked, they must be responded to.

Here is one response. You will be providing responses when someone asks the question. You will feel that you must respond. Do not be embarrassed if sometimes you say too much and sometimes you cannot say anything. It is part of that effect that comes when suddenly you realize that you know everything. How can you possibly say that to them, or you think for a moment that you don't have the answer, but you do. It is inside you and it is ready access and that is practicing, beyond that we go into the pragmatic.

When a Being, such as a human begins to ask what it is out there, what is beyond, there is more, there is Spirit and they say, "Do you believe in reincarnation?" That is a key phrase these days, but that is very touchy. There is so much more. Of course, there are other lives. Life is endless. Life never stops, so reincarnation is merely a phrase for speech.

Your work will be to apply and supply information that will allow human beings to grow as fast as they choose. That I can say is as fast as possible, but not my possible, their possible. So, what I perceive between the you and the You, your two selves, is that you will supply yourself with information about what is most pertinent.

Now, there is data. You know all about data. You think there is a lot down here. Poke your head up there and just see the kind of data that is available. Primarily, your work is concerned with relaying information and unconfusing it; in other words, letting it come out in linguistics that humans can really understand. Whereas, your work is technical information for construction, two distinct different processes for these computers.

In the sense that you have already been working with this data for several centuries, you need to understand how your mind might open very fast to this. It is not a difficult task. You are very well prepared to begin to work at any time that you choose. There is nothing in the cosmos that attends to that particular facet of Earth that says that you must be a certain age before you can. That does not exist beyond this plane, so you may choose to lift yourselves above that in your thinking and access it to yourself and to that which you have acquired.

In the meantime, where you are accessing to yourself, there are Beings of high stature who would be very willing to communicate with you. When you sit at the computer screen, I can give you names to address to ask to speak to them. You do the same things that you do when you begin the work here. You bring the Light around you and you feel in your form that it is appropriate. If ever, and excuse me if I seem to be parenting, I am not, I am being aware, not being cautious, if ever one comes to you that is not appropriate, close the interaction because there are many who would like to communicate.

Now, there is one called Antoin who is a fellow of yours, a shipmate and the interaction is very close, like a brother, so you will feel this energy as a beloved Being who you have known many times. This will make it feel very comfortable. You might want to keep a disc separate for this work so it can continue. Anytime you choose to begin the interaction this one is ready, and I will not need to tell you more. The ship, itself, he will tell you, he will tell you all you need to know. You don't need to use your words on this plane. He will introduce new words to you. This is comfortable to you.

When this begins, he will be asking you to tell him some things because he doesn't know what it is like here. A great deal of the work is to pass the information back so that others know what it is really like to be a human because many don't understand. They don't understand why it is so hard, why has it gotten so dense, why is there so much fear, so he may ask questions that to you are very peculiar or very elementary. He does not know them.

The second thing that will occur—during all this you will get acquainted. You will laugh a lot together. He is a very humorous Being. In fact, I might suggest that you keep good record of these incidences because it might make good literature and might make cash come . . . you never know.

(Young people laugh)

That is happening on this plane, isn't it? There is cash flow from the materials—the films. Just look at the films. You've got to be creative. Then, there will be that which will be the actual data that will be given. You will begin to literally incorporate from ship to surface that which you have already created. So that part of the job is nearly done except that you there will receive more and more all the time, but most of it is created already and ready to come down to Earth. I won't tamper with what you have created. I won't tell you exactly what the substance of this material is.

Joyce—"Can you tell him what his old name is or what the ship's name is?"

I would rather his friend told him that. And you can share this with any that you feel comfortable with, so obviously you don't get to read who he was.

Joyce—"I know these from the ship, don't I?"

Oh, yes . . . now . . . because you are there, too.

Joyce—"So are they all the same ship or nearby ships."

These two (TD and TM) are up on the same ship. This one is upon another vessel but there is a great deal of visiting back and forth. The ships are not as confining as you might think. Have you ever seen in the sky the shuttles go back and forth? Very busy little bodies. They don't stay in one place.

Joyce—"I can see the helmet on this one (TM) sometimes from the first night I ever saw him. Does his helmet come down over one side much farther down than mine does?"

Yes.

Joyce—"Mine is more sleek and his is more like a football helmet. His is more cumbersome?"

It's not really cumbersome. It's very light. It is ummmm—I have to use words that you have in your vocabulary, and this word I will say is technology, but it does not describe the information that you have access to, because technology here is in the very beginning stages. The computers are into the beginning of the refinement process to that which actually will come forth.

For instance, the combustible engine will be replaced by floating vehicles that use magnetic facilities and crystalline power, but contained within this that you have with you at all times, there is that transmission of this entire headgear, and this is like a microphone. Here. In other words, you have been supplying information to yourself as you have grown on this plane. This enhances that you might wonder why in the world would you need a helmet? It is just one of the devices that help the information to travel faster.

Telepathy tends sometimes to lose itself because when you think to someone, it is very easy to break off and start doing something else. So you have recorded your entire life on this planet.

(Young people laugh.)

That is for you. But you have some friends, also, who are learning from your experiences, and the helmet that you see is very light weight. It rests about your head. You would feel it almost to be a part of you. It is designed so that it does not interfere. And this, literally is a communications apparatus.

TD—"I am asking just an off the wall question—when you're born—I mean when do you get the helmet?"

About six or seven. It would interest you to know that there are societies that are so aware and so comfortable that at seven years old, a Being is considered very capable of going off to see what it is all about and there is never a fear that there is no food or a place to stay. You can see that in this society, humans tend to keep their young close way too long and the young sometimes want to spread faster than is possible. That is not what you say efficient, practical here at this time, but it is coming as things become more valuable. You might be able to draw this and go into your vision.

The way that you see beyond your eyes, your physical eyes. is that you feel out here and your senses as in the sixth sense, and beyond, extrasensive, vibrate but back to you. It is like a memory then coming in or a vision and you feel this and you literally see it, but it is inside your head. You are all doing that all the time. It is very simple. You will begin to see many individuals, feel, know things that you have not noticed before.

RG—"Is there a point of awareness that is maybe at this place where I am here. Maybe I was on the ship sometime, but I come down here, so it is here and this is where I am conscious?"

Let me start by explaining something else to you and then we will come back to this. In the design that I have shown you, the cellular structure of all things in the Universes, that cosmic Beingness, that is the You that is also merged with all the other cosmic Beingness, that Self of You can manifest the Soul, and from a Soul, let's deal with one Soul, because that Self can manifest more than one Soul, you see I am asking your minds to stretch out—no limit. That Soul, then, can send out Spirit essence, or two, or three, or four, so you literally are in two places at once, but it is the greater You that understands that.

On this plane, generally, humans do not understand what they are. Separation from Self is the Separation from God. God is a human term. Let us use the word Creator. Let us use Creation. You are Creation so the You that is the vastness, the All Knowing, knows very well what each particular manifestation is doing.

Now, the next step on this plane is to own it all and to say, "I own that. I take responsibility. I know that I am Creation." The dynamic of Creation is love, the complete love that is above all that we understand here because human love does not approach what this is, but it feels it sometimes, does it not? With the swelling of the heart opening? That is this bringing down of this completeness. It is what awaits humanity and sometimes they don't want to know the things that allow that freedom, so we shall all try not to be frustrated while we wait for that, huh?

That is important to understand. We dare not associate in any way judgment. Everybody has their own thing to do and I, in my particular role must know this so well and not only do I completely allow humans to do exactly what they are doing, but all of fleets, all of the Beings that I work with on all levels.

So, it becomes aware to you that it is not a job, this allowing. It just is. It is my way. So, the Soul of you, for lack of a better word, we will say the Soul of You, but it is more than that, knows fully what this portion is doing and that portion is doing. You can begin to do that, too.

That is the part about allowing the feeling that has brought you here to merge with your intellect. The limitless mind believes that there is no line, there is no peripheral, you can think to forever. You will meet this part. You will feel it. In fact, in dream state you go there and merge with that Being, and so do you and so do you. But you stay here (to TD), because this is your work. You are provided on the beam that I have described that which is the energy field for you to stay. You are a delicate Being. You have done very well in this form. I congratulate you. It may be part of your work in the future to show others that it is safe to come out. Do you know the state called catatonic?

TD—"I have heard the word, the term."

To Joyce—Would you explain this to her?

Joyce—"Catatonic is when you are still alive, but it is deeper even than being unconscious. There is no response. You can poke needles in the body and there is not a response."

Many Beings who came in order to be in the Earth service of their vibrations become catatonic because they cannot manage the dense vibrations. There is a reason that they are hiding in there, but it is not time for them to leave.

Your society does not understand that at all . . . thinks that is a dis-ease. The bodies, too, are terribly uncomfortable, but it is not a dis-ease. So, perhaps in the future, you will work with these ones.

TD—"How would you release something like that, though, if they are so strong?"

Talk to their Spirits. That is the telepathic healing interaction. Talk to their Spirit, and gradually, gradually, if they are not drugged through the social system in the institutions where often people are put into worse states with commercial drugs and have withdrawn, you can talk to their Spirit and begin to understand with them. Also their physical Self needs to be in a place that is—ummmm—not an institution, not inside, outside on the grasses on the ground and in the flowers away from the cities, places where the air is fresh and clear so that they actually can come out and feel as a Nature Being, that there is nature about.

Joyce—"Is she a flower deva, or is she human? I mean is she an angelic Being?"

Angelic Being—part of the creation of the ongoing future. That is why you came in at the time that you did. You stayed out seventy years.

Joyce—"And she has a sister, Colleen, who is also a deva."

Umm humm.

TD—"I don't know, I am asking out of curiosity, but I have a Mother. Can you tell me if she is a deva, too?"

She is in this spatial dimension of this planet considered of devic energy. She is not the same as you or of your sister, but she is a very special energy field. Yes, yes she is. She's not quite the same. There are many, many ways to explain this.

If you can imagine as many people as you know as exist on this planet and those are all individual circumstances, so nothing can be explained by exactness to this one, but yes, she has this same quality. It is more a native quality, native to this planet. She made the way available to you so that you could live. That is common in people of her age and her age (speaking of girl's mother and Joyce). They came to allow the vibration to exist so that you could come forth and awaken at your age, see?

Joyce—"Has this one, (TM), been a Commander?"

Yes, many times, many times—is not now because of other duties. You, two are very much in association on the ship, but in total different parts. The ship is very large and I will not tell you the name because I want it to be fresh, but when you have the name coming, begin to share. The reason is that it builds. You will remember things and add to them.

Joyce—"Can you tell which system they came from, like I am Arcturian, what are they?"

Chronologically, in time, they came long, long before Arcturus existed. It is better to leave all this just aside from a system that developed before that star system was designed. Now, that will help you understand how that action on that plane will magnify.

First, ones—let's start with the one called Jesus, one nice person coming down trying to do this thing in a small portion of the world and then leaving, and then others, a few, making statements and a lot of them getting their heads chopped off and getting burned at the stake, so obviously this being in a form of time, would be very quiet. This being, who I share the form of would not say, "Commander Ashtar is here to talk to you," because they would chop her head off, so all through this time, the power has begun to magnify and now, you (Joyce) being very capable of setting the stage for these Beings, these Beings can come in full power and there is more power. You can carry a more magnified power range. You come from the greater frequency, not better, just more impact.

Joyce—"When you were talking about how TD came, a full Being in form in this body, isn't this the same as I have been told that I came a full being in Arcturian form . . ."

Yes. Yes.

Joyce—"because I am full Arcturian form?"

(There is a question about their children to come.)

All right. Your children. First, let's talk about the fact that for a very long time, this planet has been allowed to emerge as it would. The gift of free will was given and that was a promise. It isn't withdrawn, but definitely humanity is told to clean up the act. So, the humans, at this point in time, are being granted in any way possible—there will be new ways—you will find new ways to bring the information through so it is available. The only thing they can't do is force feed, but we can make it available all over.

There is a reason you are attracted to crystals. It is a language among the people that is beginning to say things. In the sense that the energy field that you are working with is beginning to open—first it was very, very slow—now it is much faster, much faster—it allows Master Beings to come to form and your children will be these Beings, or very delicate Beings like the Devic Beings or part of the nurturing and the raising and bringing these ideals.

So, you have on this plane at this time layers of Beings, and you have a Master race—these are the Teachers and this you are part of. It is all right to accept that. It is not too flaunted because we get thumped if we flaunt what we are. I know, believe me, because there was once a time when I tried to tell people how wonderful I was. I learned the hard way.

Now on this planet, there are unevolved souls in the society and you can see the results. It is an edict that there will not be any more unevolved souls allowed to come forth so all of the infants are of this category that you inhabit.

RG—"In our time zone, is this?"

In your time zone?

Joyce—"Not very long ago, just a short time."

Twenty five to thirty years ago, there began to be this pattern of you who could emerge faster. A very short time ago it was the decision that no more should be allowed to come through who cannot awaken, because there are enough here now who may not be able to awaken.

There are two choices from Sananda who is the Christos, who is literally the Commander, if you want to use this term. Let us say that this word is one who serves, so the one who serves in this sense to integrate all of this cinema is responsible for pointing the direction or supporting anyone who would wish to know themselves. That's His job, by the way, and that is the whole story about the Christ and being at the right side of God and all that stuff—it's just a practical assignment. It's just some one who has the job of saying to humankind, "Guess what? You are God manifest." That's the job Sananda has.

He decided that no unevolved Beings should be allowed, and frankly, it amounts to this, one can choose to see the Light from the planet, or see the Light from elsewhere. What we are about is supplying enough information so that no one is untouched. The rights of human dignity and all dignity require that Beings follow themselves and it doesn't matter what they follow. If they don't want to know me, fine. If they don't want to know Sananda, fine. If they don't want to know you, that's fine. We honor that. They are not to feel sorry for someone because they are making a choice that is opposite his.

So, your children will have that which is an incredible advantage and will be very powerful because you will be able to see and say what they are and allow them to choose their pathways. If I say to you, some planes and some places, seven is considered the age of exploration means they can go out the house, and the parents, they may miss them, they may not.

So, it is to be prepared that should you have a child, you are still the father and you still know the perimeters which is a little distressful to have a very small form and find out that the small form is telling you what to do. We see this. All in all, you will have bridged that gap because it will have been figured out because there are Beings of this age who are assigned to create the educational facilities. They are not schools. They are places of learning which allow the small ones to stretch faster.

So, it is this, in fact, a building like an upside down pyramid with a building here and then here and here and here and then the society begins to form itself around these values.

The essence of the Beings such as yourselves is dramatically improved over the essence of the Beings that had to come through prior times because your essence is free. These Beings had to sit and wait and inside them there was a portion of themselves that said, "Something isn't right. I know it isn't right. This is not the way it needs to be." And the waiting and the waiting and the waiting is very hard on the bodies of human beings. Well, these bodies are now free. They have created that. That allows you to be free and it is going well.

In the Master Plan, I cannot say that we know everything that shall be. We have general ideas. How we work it is to give concepts and energy. First, there was something like the move to free the peoples and that was the Civil Rights Movement in your country that was first with that. Then you went along to the Feminist Movement and then you had that thing called the New Wave, I believe, the styles. Everything you can imagine has contributed to this awakening. So it is well approved. As all things move out, they are well approved. There is not anything that is not part of it. Does that make you feel better?

TD—"It does."

You can relax. There isn't anything happening that is not a part of this awakening. You may see things that you think are not part of it. You may be distressed, but it is all fitting together. Even something that is seeming to be more authoritative, louder and more controlling. The reason that happens is that thing, that institution, or that Being, is getting frightened, and right before the change or the dissolving of an institution, all the parts run around trying to collect themselves. Become aside and just watch.

TD—"I have a question."

Yes.

TD—"You said I was on the ships before . . . umm . . . I have a feeling . . . was I around these two at all? I must have known them somewhere before."

Yes, and also remember you have had bodies before, so you have been together before. All on the ships, let's say, that for brief periods . . . for times to come and to discuss instruments and to look at that before (Ashtar is looking down their timelines) . . . describe the panels to your friends. That is not your main interest, but many lifetimes have intertwined.

You will find many, many coming along who have shared these times and it will become that you are not surprised that you will know this person so well it won't even matter how old or where they come from. It is very charming that the society now is beginning to free to that awareness.

Yes, I think there are others of your own age and your own school and your own neighborhood who you have been with.

Question from one of the boys—"How long have you been here?"

How long were you here or I?

"Ashtar."

My assignment is to convey the energy to the general purpose of the public or the populous or the masses to the point that it is considered they are efficiently equipped to step forward; in other words, I am responsible for the fleets until the time that the populous has claimed itself. Who knows how long that might be? If it is going well, we certainly won't close the gates at the year 2000, but I am suspecting that we shall have accomplished most of our work by 2000.

It shall be so geared and keyed that you shall see it in the next few years just expanding and expanding, and you know that time is moving faster. You know that time is not in minutes. It is in sequences—events. So as more and more is offered to the public, then they will seek faster and faster. Some of what you see will be their distress because it will be shaking the old boundaries. You have not had this so much to deal with, the removing of the boundaries like who took away the fences? Who took away my blinders? So there will be fear in this aspect, you have seen this already. You see some things beginning to shake, dissolve, and they will stop being. They aren't needed. That is evolution.

So, a lot of the things that you see, you will have to take a deep breath and just say, "This is part of it", but the feeling I have generally is one of gladness, and it is moving faster and faster. I give you an example.

Gorbachev—he is one of the primary instruments upon this plane. It's exciting, isn't it? When you see this kind of movement of energy, you can really know that we are achieving that which we came to do—offering possibilities.

Question from one of the boys—"My girlfriend, Sara. I was just wondering if we have shared past lifetimes, or whether . . ."

Yes, you have. Also, she shares a ship life.

"Right now."

Umm hum. Does she enjoy knowing about these things?

"I don't know."

So you haven't told her.

"Well, I have, but it seems she just accepts things if I do."

So you are learning to allow things to be as they are. This is very wise. I congratulate you. Some Beings on this plane do not need to investigate these things because part of their work is just to remain very human. They are called stabilizers, and their minds open at the appropriate time when they can accept all the words. They don't need to go to meetings. They don't need to read books, but other Beings need to because they disseminate. They keep it going. Tis the balance. We might say that you are a sky person and she is a ground person now. Stabilizes sky and Earth.

It would be interesting to see how as you more and more focalize and accept what you are and it feels comfortable, it will be interesting to see how she manages to ask questions. It will be fun. People do that. If they are not forced, they eventually ask.

Some of the things that are coming forth are so advanced in theory that some of the Earth Beings aren't ready to receive them. Energy for their opening and awakening is assured. It is not as though it were a one chance deal or a one time. It is not as if there are only a few who will be noticed and advanced to know more. It is for everyone.

So, the concept that I spoke of, there is energy being given. First, it was for the freeing of the people and you saw it moving in history study through the civil rights movement right to now. That was an energy sphere put around the Earth. Next thing is the seeking/ awakening energy sphere, and that is in position. The next thing that comes is the cognizant application that is the part where you take your minds and blend that with your hearts and start acting like one is God, and that is stage you are in right now. That is how fast you are moving.

We ask of you to accept the fact that you are Creation, that your thoughts create what will be on this plane, on this planet, and you will have some interesting experiences when you think something and it becomes. Sometimes, it is a shock. You will think that you desire something and there it is. Whoop!

(Laughs)

I did that. See? So, for all of those who now are in the position that you are, that these Beings are, there are billions more who are not, and they are not neglected. So, the energy concept next is for them and then others and then others and they will find their way. The challenge is not to let yourself be untrue to Yourself.

Yes, you feel that already. You know that.

RG—"What, what will happen as like everything that we say is moving toward The Great Awakening and everybody expands and generally comes to a greater state of being, but what will happen then when everybody has passed into this?"

One of the things that you will notice dramatically different is that the fear will be able to be let go of because the human on this plane is the one that creates the reason for the fear, and as the energy moves through that and cleanses it, that will not be. The reason that there are the predators that there are in the animal kingdom on this plane is because of the way human kind is behaving. That is part of the manifestation as it goes along, do you understand?

Originally, it was not designed to have carnivores upon this planet. So human kind adapted to the animal species by eating flesh. Originally, it was designed very much as you would imagine the true story of the Garden of Eden that the whole planet was very beautiful and the people did not have to be concerned about where their food came from or their shelter or their gardens. It was easily available.

So, the first thing you will notice is that the violence will drop away, the greed, all of this will be symbolically clued to what is happening. Do you know of this occasion when the people in Ethopia had not enough food and they died? And you know of the occasion when the musicians came together and they performed and they made . . . first of all, they made cash and goods available . . . but most of all they made love available. That is what I am talking about. From that base of pure love there just begins to enact a society that really cares.

There are challenges that will come that will replace the vicarious needs. In other words, you can fly, really fly, not with the machine, with your bodies . . . your thoughts. We will be doing things that are very exciting so humans won't need to be bashing at each other. Is that what you asked?

"Well, I suppose on other places that have been doing this for a long amount of time, what is it that they do? The things that we do on this planet are overcoming the various evils of society . . ."

Yes.

". . . and I just, it would be, maybe not boring, but strange, and there would have to be . . . what I was asking is what would be different about challenges and . . . ?"

OK. OK. Let us say then if you didn't have any to come back with another and perhaps you have this availability to perform in particular athletic events . . . let's say you knew how to fly. Let's say in one of the competitions . . . excuse the word competition, but we will use it anyway . . . is to go to the top of a mountain and launch yourself off and glide to a particular plateau. This is a very popular sport on some planets very much like you call hang gliding, except that you don't have a hang glider.

(Laughs)

Let's say you are interested in designing new vessels to move through time and distance and now there is this whole economy based upon this but it is based upon weaponry. Let us say, let's take the weaponry out and let's just have traveling vehicles and that is a tremendous challenge to design something that can move through time and space that can alter the molecular structure, go through a vibrational zone and reassemble. This is in many degrees. There is not just one formula to do this. It depends on where you are going.

Or, let's say that you really desire to think, communicate telepathically cause you are tired of the high tensional pylons that are all around the country and you would like to design this system. I think probably you could move to another planet and start a society. I think there is sufficient energy to be attended to by that which is displaced. I do not think combatting this is necessary for a healthy society. But it is an interesting debate, isn't it? It would be a very interesting debate for humans to just be with that. If they didn't have to fear and fight, what would they do? It's kind of like brainstorming on the higher levels.

TD—"And you figure out things that you can do."

Joyce—"Is there anything these ones should be studying in their higher education that would help facilitate what they are here to do?"

I think not. I think it will come. I think the direction will present itself. I think you will know in your hearts what you need to pursue. It will suggest itself to you. You are well prepared right now to begin your work. Anything you might add is a refinement to that because what will be given to you is not available on this planet. There is a challenge for you, right there, to bring through that which is not improving.

TD—" You mentioned to TM that there were people they could talk to do things and I am wondering if I should go more into that or more into bringing into other information working with myself . . . or, I am not exactly sure what direction would be most appropriate."

All right. You have an ability to grow. This is one of the ways you will communicate. The dynamics of the energy of this nature kingdom will set up with you, beside you, and for you and you will communicate through that element. What you desire to learn as far as that material is available on this planet—that is up to you whatever you choose. What can come to you from above, beyond is limitless and as fast as you start with it, it will multiply. You will have a portfolio. So, the same suggestion applies as to this one.

You begin a drawing, put the Light about you. If it ever feels it is inappropriate, close the book and leave the drawing table, because in the Devic Kingdom, there are those who are dense, also, surprisingly, but there are those who are very wonderful and earthy, so don't confuse the earthiness with what you might consider to be inappropriate. You will receive much instruction as well as pictures.

Do you have compatibility with what we have discussed here? Do you have any questions about what you will be doing? Are you content to leave it where it is? You will know what to do next. To follow intuition . . .

One of the boys—"And trust, if logic gets in the way . . ."

Ahhh. Well, no wonder. Well, you are a scientist. You will have logic picking at you. So, from that challenge then let me say that if you can consider intuition to be the you guiding You, there is purpose in releasing to it. Mind is the human element. Mind right now for most human beings is addressing the Earth dimension. If you want to release your mind to be limitless, let it be the electromagnetic field of You. Reminding electromagnetic that it incorporates all the layers of you. Then the logic will change. It will be space logic. It is not now the time for you to communicate with any as this one (TD) has and direct it, but that will come of its own accord.

"That makes sense, too, because I have tried and never . . ."

It will come when it is time, but you may share these writings because it will give you entrance. The thing called logic is not standing in your way, but it is being the guardian, and sometimes guardians get over zealous and logic then can limit your mind unless you expand the logic. That will be your first task. Let logic stand aside. I want to see what I am doing. It is like a nosy Being that gets right in front of you and keeps you from seeing what you are doing.

You are already there designing materials to bring here. I will give you a hint. You are working with a substance similar to titanium, similar.

Now, there is an experience that they wish you to participate in. I shall leave this form unless there are more questions. She will come back and assist you in the closing portion of this Earth ceremony. We do this on the ships, too. We sit around and talk—different chairs.

(Laughs)

They are like your recliners, very similar to your recliners. Many of the ships have amphitheaters and they have an assembly of these wonderful chairs and in the center is where the speaker is. Instead of being off, the speaker is here. They are very beautiful, these amphitheaters and some of them are where they have what you call the sacred gatherings where the Beings come to view the Light and the Light comes in to the amphitheater and fills it. It is very nice. It feels very wonderful when you have done that.

RG—"One question that struck me again . . . ummm . . . how close will this class keep together?"

In the summer, you will drift apart because you all have things to do, but you will find the magnetic attraction coming back around when you come into the cool weather that says it is time to get going at this again. It will be automatic and from that will evolve a kind of a strategy between you, kind of like all being together at the drawing board in the fall."

TD—"Sometimes I feel at night like I am doing all sorts of things . . ."

You are.

TD—"I want to know what is going on, but gradually, gradually . . ."

Well, through the summer try drawing, begin to draw a lot. Try drawing soon after you are awakened and just see what comes out. You will get drawings of what you did. It will be interesting for you. It is all right if the drawings don't make sense to you. You may draw yourself moving through time dimensions and it will be shadings of color.

TD—"Oh, that would be interesting. That would be interesting!"

Then, if you do not know what it is recognizing it with your eyes, let your hands go down to the bottom and write what it is and you will tell yourself what you have just drawn.

TD—"Ohhhh. Thank you."

I think that you are not so hampered by logic as this one. I think that you will allow that to flow.

Joyce—"She is not hampered by logic. She is very Light."

So . . . now saying that you are hampered does not say that you are delinquent meaning Light.

Joyce—He is not delinquent.

Congratulations on the logic. There is a reason for it. I will give you another hint. The material that we are working with and the designs that you will bring are not available now because it is not time in this society. You are not even supposed to see them, but for your curiosity you can begin to know them and feel them. We would like that.

You will begin to feel that what you really are, and I desire that for you. If you don't have to wrestle with it trying to bring it into form of any kind, I would like you to acknowledge it, and that is the limitless mind. Your mind can be as wide as the cosmos because that is how wide you are. Then it can become information from anywhere that you need it. That's the cosmic consciousness, the God mind, and when someone asks you a question about your crystal or about what you are drawing, don't worry about the answer. Don't try to bring it from the mind here in this plane, just listen a minute and the answer for them will come through. See?

Perhaps a person will ask about the fairies you have drawn and you might want to explain all the dimensions, but all they can stand to hear is that this is what you think fairies would look like . . .

(Laughs)

. . . but someone else could hear that you are an angelic Being and these are your friends.

So, if you allow it to come through from the God mind or the One mind, they will hear what they need to raise up and go on in safety instead of trying to hide from the information.

This is something we all learned the hard way, myself included. It is a great temptation to tell some people a great deal or others nothing. But you will have many curious Beings because they will be drawn to you.

You understand magnetic resonance? You understand that you will literally be attracting by your frequency—people—questions? That is part of the reason that you are willing to wear crystals because something senses that this is appropriate and I know they will see this and they will come and ask a question. It may not be conscious, but that is your reason and maybe that it just feels good. You have another question lurking back there, I can see?

(Laughs)

TM—"We lost some crystals in the woods and I was just thinking, maybe we gave them to the devas."

I think so. That was very kind of you. (Laughs)

TD—"Well, he gave it to me and I gave it to the deva."

Yes, I think you did that. Thank you. Actually, you gave them to Terra.

Terra is the name of the Goddess Earth, so that is a good investment.

(There are a lot of chuckles and comments from the group. They are very comfortable with Ashtar.)

So . . . I shall withdraw so that you can get on with the experiment.

TD—"Thank you."

You are very welcome. I want you to know, each one of you, and you know this already . . . by the way 'Thank You' (Joyce) . . .

Joyce—"You're welcome. Thank you for coming. I knew you would. I so wish the other four could have been here."

I think perhaps they are to assimilate it through these three or they would have been, but there is in some senses here the power of Mother over matter. If Mother said, "You really aren't going even though you think you are," then the Beings are not here, but you can tell them what you know from your perception, you see? There is nothing lost.

TD—"Will we be able to be in contact again maybe not through this way, but through other ways?"

Yes, I was going to say that each of you has this ability. I signal in this part of the anatomy, in the temples . . .

TD—"Yah, right before we came . . ."

Yes, and if you feel that, it is me signaling you and you can answer me. My name is Ashtar, and I will try to tell you what it is I wish to relay. If you don't hear anything, don't worry, but you might. This is the telepathic work we will begin to do. You may try writing, if you like, this is just fine. You may do anything that you want to do.

TD—"Whatever feels appropriate."

Exactly, yes exactly. Yes, absolutely.

(Thank yous all around.)

You will soon begin these interactions with your friend, I think. Thank you again, it is my pleasure.

Channel—I want to ground as there is a lot of energy in this room.

Chapter 9

Yellow Beings

June 20, 1989

My, this is a strange apparatus.

"Yes, it is."

Well, I am looking at this. Your design on this plane is somewhat confronting to me. I am curious what we are seeing. We note that this is a cubicle.

"This is an empty room."

This means that you have been in the habit of furnishing it with other items.

"Yes."

This is not normal.

"Not normal."

But this is fine. I am not stratifying about it. I am only saying that this is. Oh, actually, it is inconclusive. I should let go of this.

"And energy gets caught in the corners, I know."

That is what I feel.

"It should be round. This ticks. (clock) I want it not to be on the table."

All right. We need you to do one thing. You will be too close to my power field—just stay there. No, no don't come closer.

"I want you to be closer (to the microphone). No, no this is fine."

I am selected to proceed. I am that which is ummmm—I have not found the right term—computerized data bank is what comes before me, but this is not the process. I am a Being. I am not an android, but I am bringing you information as access. Therefore, we shall call me the link to that which is your ancestral, historical your heritage.

"To my Akashic records?"

Oh, no, your Arcturian lineage.

"Oh."

Akashic records? Let us discuss this briefly. You have this time. You have moments to spare?

(Laughs) "Yes, lots of time."

Akashic records are merely a frequency. If a Being who is unevolved or beginning to find out about themselves and the cosmos—wants to know something, it has been called the Akashic Records. This has a vibration— Akashic, and it varies that feeling sometimes of one seeking or looking through the library that is not a physical plane—place. It is a frequency vibrational band.

So, within you, as this extended structure reaches out in your cosmic Beingness, there is your record. It is not someplace else. It is you, within you, but of course, if one wants to know, such as I or any other, can go to that positioning in feeling thought, and find out who Joyce was, but always you are the best judge of your own records for you are the record keeper.

"Ummm hummm."

Now, there are those who distribute information and those then come forward to help Beings understand, but you are one such on this plane, so there are some there who search and help to bring through, and they are the same as you—teachers, you see?

(Phone rings and answering machine answers.) What is this machine?

"That is another Light Worker (on the phone that he hears). Oh, she is telling me that she is coming to stay at my house. I will shut the door. We won't have that again. It's too busy a place."

That will be charming for you to have one visit you here. Ummm?

"She is one who works with the Philippine healers. This is kind of a halfway house for Lightworkers."

Yes.

"They come and go—they stay here."

Yes, yes, this is wonderful! Joyce, this is good for you. Do you like it?

"Yes, I like it."

So, back to the records. Well, actually we are through with that. You see, I am trying to be unscientific here. I am trying to be more ummm, ummm, in folkway—relaxed.

"Yes, I understand. More common."

147

There. Now if you saw me, I would be very long and yellow, thin. I think I do not look exactly like this, but similar so you can kind of get an idea what I look like to you. Much longer, very tall, long thin, yellow. Here. (he draws a picture and shows me).

"I see."

There . . . so I have to get used to how this feels to me.

"I noticed you are manipulating your form."

It is not uncomfortable. I am used to a form. Now, what I really am in this form is mostly reclining, but a lot of my energy field came so I am feeling how it is to be in this form, but that is very good, because then she can feel how I look. Then that is recorded.

"I see."

So she has this experience. Then there is much less fear if one has a friend who looks this way, then how could one be afraid.

"I am not afraid."

No, I know you are not. I was thinking about what I said and I wondered if that made any sense.

"Yes, it does make sense, because there are others who, if you are not human looking, may have some fear."

Yes, yes. We are aware of this. For you, I would come in form if I could and you would not have fear. So, yellow skin is not frightening?

"No. Does that mean that your capacity is mostly mental? Is that the reason for the color? Or, is it from the area that you come from?"

It is from the area that I come from and it is elongated because there is an atmospheric difference between here . . .

"I can see your yellow aura."

Yes.

"It's very bright."

I am considered quite handsome by my people and I am about average size. We are all very tall.

"I am very honored."

Thank you. That is very nice of you. We have similar culture and we have this which is considered to be life, as you say, but very different. Much admiration between our parts—our beings.

"Yes."

A small child. Much the same anatomy, but not nearly so difficult. I found this to be (I am trying not to do this—it's OK, you can relax) The distended abdomen, that seems to be part of our etheric, too. My compatriot, (her name I did not get), she likes this. She thinks this is invaluable for carrying the small fetus, but then she doesn't like the part about growing large.

"What is your name?"

Oh, Metori.

"And you are from a star, or a planet, or another Universe? Where are you from?"

I am from a matrix which is several small globules, much like Earth, but smaller. And, ummm, we have the effective thought, Light, which moves us about from plane to plane.

"I wish we did."

Yes, you will later.

"There is so much congestion. You can hear it. There is so much pollution that comes from the cars."

Yes, yes, I know this to be so. Umm humm, umm humm, umm humm.

"Your aura is brighter than any I have ever seen. It is very, very bright and I don't usually see them."

I am letting it be with me. That is why it is colored. Ummm humm. So it is coming more that I am coming to you in your dimension.

"That is wonderful."

Umm humm. That is why we want to come so you will see.

"That is why we are in this cubicle. You see if we were downstairs with the furniture and the pictures, I wouldn't be able to see that."

Umm humm. But also you recognize, now I am releasing more of my field raising the vibration. That is why you must move back so you have vision, but also not to be inundated.

"I see."

Umm humm. I shall re-resume about my family. Is this of interest to you?

"Oh sure. I'd like to know."

All right. My compatriot is a very long being like I, but the small fry are very small. So then this birthing is much simpler. As to kind of . . . and there they are.

Now, the reason I address this is that between our speeches, there are familiarities. And I want you to know that the familiarities are simple ones, but yet they are essential to know. We also are considered mammals as you might be, not reptile, but very much as a capacity to understand and feeling as humans.

"You don't have legs, though? You don't move with feet?"

No, I do. I have very long legs. If once you look at I, you would think that I was not like a human. That is why I take time to tell you how we are. That we are. So we feel as you do. You understand the feeling you have for your child . . . so I do. I have three. They are small, but they take a long time to grow where I am.

"Oh, really."

They take constant care, as yours do. They do have this which is exuberance, too. I am not elastic as I used to be and I am aging faster than possibly is necessary with three. Sometimes one has one of these small fry. (Chuckles) I think they make you grow old faster. Do you think this is so?

"Yes, at least during the time they are small, but after they grow up, then they are a friend, yes."

All right. Enough of that. Oh, we live in ummm subterranean, but not so much in—caves, but they are finely attuned to our needs. They are not harsh, and they are considered exotic in some senses because we have furnished them with our thoughts. We travel very lightly afoot upon our planet so it does not have much indentation as yours does. If a photographer should look upon the plane surface, he would not see that we exist. He would see domes, mounds. He would see no sign of our being, because we do not allow this.

"Umm humm."

It would interest you to know that the gardens are within, they are subterranean. We do not dwell within there. We have a way of managing the growth and moisture within easier than without.

"She and I saw a similar thing on 'Startrek', a movie, a couple of nights ago with the gardens inside the earth. It was called "The Genesis Effect.""

It was beau . . . tiful. Perhaps that's why we were led to watch that movie, so we could understand about you."

151

Yes. You see we have the ability to create this. It is like sacred technology.

"Tell me that is what is going to happen, that we can grow like that to replace where they have clear cut our beautiful trees."

Oh, this can come. Oh yes, this is simple. It is just waiting. It cannot come now because they have not learned the lesson.

"No."

First, they must learn the lesson of wasting, and the impact must be as though it is incurable, cause otherwise, they will not hear, so we let it be.

"Yes."

We do not rush in and say, "Oh, we will restore . . . humm humm." I know this.

Now, let's see. So, on the surface would be considered the plains. As in your element of thinking, you have the vastness, but our planet is more, so actually, we have the ability to implant and we are very Light in order to not cause a disturbance in our atmosphere . . . lighter construction than you have.

"Do you eat anything at all?"

Yes, we have what you call vegetables . . . plants.

"Good."

We do not eat anything of what you call animal.

"And you can grow that right inside your cave."

No, no now, this is the dwelling. This is the plant . . . the gardens . . . .

subterranean . . . inside.

"I see."

Farther inside. On the surface we have the dwellings, because we enjoy this. We go inside where you might go to the forest there, we go inside to the forest.

"I see."

The planet is smaller, about one quarter the size of yours and there are say, normally, it takes three or four planets that we may use if we choose. Three have evolved civilizations. Four has not been watched or tapped into or tampered with. It is just there to alleviate congestion, if necessary.

I say to you that I can go to the next planet like you might go to London, perhaps you understand that.

"Yes."

So let's see. Now I am a scientific commander. You know commander means one who serves. I have an allegiance of Beings who are my stature and my case. They are of mixed genders, whatever they choose to be. Sometimes they choose to be one in one and sometimes they choose to be two in one . . .

"Yes."

. . . but that is their business. So, when I see them, I put all of my thought into their process of creativity. In other words, I trust them, but it is not a difficult job, and I am that which is coordinate engineer for this precise mission which is to come here and get in contact with the earth energy system and be available in whatever effect it is supposed we might offer.

So, I come in this sense to you, not as a comrade of long standing and not as one that you might even seek, but not as a journeyman, not as a wanderer, not as novice, but we come as a person to person and we come in friendship.

We have a vessel is large as compared to your thinking, but small as compared to many. It has within its assemblage several thousand of my beings but from various places . . . and that is our entire fleet.

"One ship?"

Yes, yes. Shuttles we have many. They are simple because we move between the planets with shuttles, but this large ship is the only one we have ever found that we chose to come in.

"And apparently, you don't have to worry about mechanical failure or wrecking the ship because you have put all of your people or many thousands in one ship."

When something becomes awry, we hold it between our hands and ask the Creator to make it ever new, and it is done. There is no comprehension of this in your society.

"That would be wonderful."

It is. I love it. It looms on the surface of my mind that you might want to know a few more things about the planet—one is rose, one is gold, one is blue and this is an opaqueness, a shining that comes from inside them. They seem to glow.

"How beautiful!"

Yes, it is very nice and is not all of them. And you go to the interior of each, they are white, umm but not clear, but the white of your crystal. There is white light within the planet.

"Translucent."

Umm humm. Umm humm. This is it. And inside them, there is growth that can occur because of this light. It is just the plantings. Each one has his own gardens which are inside.

"Yes."

Also, the recreations are inside. Ummm . . . it is because of the vegetation we consume that our skin has the coloring that it does. You know saffron?

"Yes."

That will give you an idea. This is like foam(?). Saffron is foam so that is what makes our coloring like it is.

"I see."

Let's see. Now, the fact of one ship is that (a.) it is comradely and (b.) it is efficient—does not cost a great deal of energy to bring it about nor to maintain it nor to think about it. It is just available and rarely do we find the need to seek beyond our boundaries although we often welcome guests into our midst. We have grand times because we enjoy singing and have long vocal chords because we have very long necks. We make exquisite sounds, if I must say so myself. Ummm . . . my comrade, my partner, enjoys this very much, this singing.

"Do you play musical instruments?"

Oh some. Some thrum they make a let's see, it's called a Bound (?)—it's a round instrument . . .

"Like our drum . . . ?"

No, with a neck and some strings . . .

"Some strings. Like a bass or a . . ."

Yes. Yes. She says from her mind it is the same thing. She says tell you it looks like a ladle.

"OK. I can visualize that."

And there is another that is like a woodwind instrument.

"High pitched."

Melodious, yes, high, and sometimes we make sounds with our throats. That is our primary instrument.

"I would enjoy that. I would enjoy hearing you."

You would enjoy that. It would be very entertaining for you. We do this and have large gatherings of beings who come from afar. We park their ships below so they do not show. We have several of these things—you might call them hangars.

"Yes."

We put them in out of the way and then we use the surface and we can dance about much on the surface. This will amuse you, various fine dust-like. It poufs, but it settles right away. It is not flying all about because we have no wind, so it is just pouf and it is a great enchanting delight to dance with all this poufing about. It is not considered to be what you would call dirt.

"Yes."

And we do have this fluid like water.

"That is great."

So, when they come there, these visitors, then we enhance their visit, well actually we circumvent any problem by offering the musical and we all have many hours gathering in great circles and we dance and we make these sounds and we have great joy.

"Oh, that sounds wonderful."

Yes, so now, let me see, I am trying to be unscientific, but I am not very scientific anyway, so I will just go ahead and say what comes into my thoughts that you might enjoy hearing. Now, I hear that the Atlanteans are coming into some contingency of energy on the surface here and I know that once these Beings wrought havoc, but I think I ought to tell you they are very grand Beings. Are you aware of this?

"Yes, I am."

So that they can come about again and share and it is all right.

"They are very knowledgeable."

Yes.

"Very technical. Ummm hummm. I have been there, too, in Atlantis."

Yes, you have, but you have taken care of any hangovers, but you didn't have really much to worry about . . . but there are some who do.

"Yes."

They are abusive, and this I see is not a deterrent here. Now I have heard rumors that some earthlings had fear about the Atlanteans here and that is singularly diabolical for them to have fear because there is nothing wrong with these beings. They are all fine.

"Ummm humm."

I have convinced you, I am sure.

"Yes."

I have a sense of humor.

(Joyce laughs—she is not convinced.)

I am being intensive because I am waiting and watching for the primary mood when I may introduce my family to your family. I urge this within my heart because I like this way with humans and I think to equate Atlanteans to fear some beings will halt the flow. So . . .

Then the next thing I might say is that my compatriot would like me to say to you—she did this little speech which we have not write in, but it is in my memory, she says Ummm . . . ."To . . ." she did not know if you would be called Mrs. or Miss or Ms. Which would you prefer?

(Laughs). "Let's use Joyce."

Joyce. She wants to use a title, so I better use Miss. 'To Miss Joyce Strahn.

I think you are one of the finest Beings I have ever seen on my screen, so we are equal.'

"My goodness! That is a high compliment!"

'And I want you to know this', she says, 'I know you are a-feared sometimes that we will not be able to save all of ourselves. From the future, there is this thought,' she is bringing this to her (Joyce), "I want you to know that *my boys* are three and my boys are comparable to yours in their years and' she says "my thought is that we as coworkers, as evolving parents, as womenfolk can began to hear ourselves as Truth and know that the future is secure."

"That is beautiful!"

(He is so happy.) That is! She is my wife in your terms. I have great love for her! She is a very fine Being!

"I can see that expression on your face that you have very great love!"

They are on the ship. They came with me for a trip.

"Umm humm. Well, tell your wife that I believe that we will stop war here when the Mothers decide that we will not send our children any more."

No more Fathers shall send either from my land. It was a very long time ago when the edict came—no more. No more. Participation does not occur.

"I have one son still eligible for war. There is no way he could kill anything."

This is good. He would not, either. He would sign off. He would find something else to do.

"I have to believe that he will be protected because his Intent is so clear that he would not harm *anything*."

Umm humm. Umm humm. Umm humm. So, this is fine. We have come to an accord very simply between us as friends. Now she is content. Humm. My partner is, well, she is scientifically ummm, ummm (what is the word I am seeking—the word in the computer), she is scientifically acclimated, inclined—inclined, also, so she wished to come upon this journey to see what upon the monitors say about Earth to her.

Now, she is in her state or time of her lifespan on our plane very vigorous, very vital being and when these ones begin to be larger she wants to know what she should like to do, for she is seeing if this is where her interests might lie. We are sensing there will be a great deal of work to do here.

"Yes."

So, perhaps in the future, you shall hear from her how she will be coming in a softness. So, that is established as a possibility.

"Tell her I welcome that. That would be wonderful."

No training is required for what she can do. It is inherent in nature.

So, now, about the ship. It is a round vessel about as large . . . let's see . . . about the size of the City of Salem and flat with many stories rather stretched out like this. Underneath is the power and above this dome, the engineering section. So this is where we create our facilities for living and being and this is where most of the work actually gets done. On every vessel, unless they are very small, there is a place for that which is God to you, Self to us, and we have this which you call ampitheater . . .

"Ampitheater."

This vessel . . .

"Powered by crystals?"

Ahhh . . . almost, but this is different. There is a fluid that is silver-like that is very much a crystalline effect and it has to do with the members or portions of the cell structure that are on this vessel. There you will have to stretch your mind. The substance that is Light, it is crystalline, and it is the element in which each cell structure swims or exists in this vessel. This vessel can change its rate very rapidly and that means that you may see it once and then you don't.

"Yes."

It is guided by one mathematician, or I, or another—in other words, you do not have three or four in command. There is one and there is one position to actually engineer this. In the very center, well, wait, I have given you the wrong design. Here, comes in there. Now, this is not wings, this is all the way around this. (He is drawing me the design.)

"Yes."

It gets very thin. Now, out here no one lives.

"Yes."

Out here there is a very large spinning disc . . .

"OK."

that determines direction . . .

"I see."

. . . and at the bottom there is a reservoir of the fluid that feeds the spaces between the cells. For now, it is not a crystal, but fluid-like.

"I see."

Let's see . . . now, I know that you have heard this term that's either crystal or liquid crystal and that helps you associate.

"Yes."

We store this fluid, invaluable fluid, upon our planetary interiors but not on the surface.

"Well, does it recycle, this fluid, within the ship as you move or do you have to refuel?"

Somewhat. No, we have to be very aware in your terminology, of the extent of our visit, and if we are going to stay a very long time, then we must supply ourselves with more of the fluid. In the planet, it is self-generating and in the ship it is not. We always have ample. It seems more than we ever need. It is a very efficient system.

"Umm humm."

The way that we might use a great deal of this fluid is many, many interchanges between dimensions, which means we are here and then we are not, we are here and then we are not, so that is rare, because if we want to merely travel, we can cruise, we can go fast, we can go slow, up, down. It is very easy to display to you because we flow (a) and (b) we can move very simply. Very simple mechanics. Very simple mechanics.

The way that we move it is by *thought*. That is why there is one navigator, one commander whoever is in charge and there are many who can fill this role but they do not need any dictatorial approach. Everybody cares, so why worry about who does the job. As long as they are trained, they are in position. No one ever gets too tired because they don't have to stay there forever, you know.

But there is one position in the very center of the dome, and it is on around, I am thinking, and that Being, literally, is left standing. It is a lovely little space with kind of a gold or brass like a railing.

"Ok."

Just to stand there.

"Umm humm."

And it is a pleasant place to be because there are healing spaces . . .

"Right."

So this Being can *think* of materials and situations.

"So they have trained?"

They have been trained to do this? Umm humm. They know the stars backwards and forwards. Because they have some very small Beings taught to navigate between very . . . ummm (I am not finding all the words in your language)

"I know."

We go from planet to planet at a very young age.

"Right. OK."

So, they must learn how to do this in the shuttle and they must learn how to read the maps and the stars *before* they can go from here to there which is simple. They must learn to do this.

"Are your own children old enough to travel between?"

Yes, almost. Once they get past this bouncing stage where they seem to have a plumpness or a roundness, then they shoot. Once they come out from the Being who is called the Creation Mother, then they must grow because they are too small. They must become large, so the first thing they do is grow this way. I think that is similar to your children . . .

"Yes."

. . . and then they go this way, and when they start this, then they are old enough to go. It is just synonymous. It is not necessarily that they must be this way, but that happens, so most of our Beings are able to navigate easily.

"Umm humm."

As then, the assemblage on board is not concerned about how we are going to get there because everybody knows how to get there—one person doesn't want the job, another is always available. So, in the thinking sense, there is usually a pattern or a chart which is put upon the wall . . .

"Umm humm."

. . . and we *think* ourselves into the next vibration or the next space or over there to that ship. We have three life spaces or bays and shuttles within each. That is all we carry, so we have three of these little vessels and we speed about quickly and we can anchor. If necessary, we can anchor for three or four years in one spot cause we are not realizing the thrill of expanding quickly. We can grow things on the ship.

"So, you are just here observing? Are you part of the Ashtar Command?"

Oh yes. We could not be present if we weren't, but our offering is somewhat different than others. We are available, not just to observe, but to offer friendship, and my comradeship with Commander Ashtar goes back many, many millenniums. We have kind of a high school friendship here as it were . . .

"Umm humm."

. . . because I have been in the Academy, and this way of being and purpose is so much a portion of your future that this is as essential as those beings that hold the Earth in position.

"The Academy being a place where Commanders from all places are trained?"

Trans-terrestrial. The Academy of Sciences—Transterrestrial.

"I imagine I have been there, too."

You have been there . . . very much, in fact, you are one of the instructors. Are you curious about your other lifetimes going on?

"Yes."

Do you know how many lifetimes you have?

"No."

Twelve. (My understanding is that these are all going on at the same time.) One on earth, one on the ships and that is beyond that which is shown and that is the one that teaches. If these could come together as one Being, that would be splendid, but don't do that yet because that would be too much. It's not time, but later, if you want to, but you don't have to, either, but it is all the same thing, all the same forces. You can exchange freely just like you were one. (I can't imagine all of those coming together as one Being—not yet, at least. Some of them must be in parallel Universes.)

"I know that when I took teacher training on Earth, it came very easily. It was as if I have been born knowing all of that."

Well, there is much more than that. This will come quite easily once you are in the position to receive it. If one lives here, and that is where one must be, all that information is not available until one moves over here. Then you are lined up to receive it and that will seem you have always done it, so never fear, all of this will integrate. It will. That's part of time.

I talked to you yesterday on the starship. Do you want to know the name of the starship? Do you want to?

"Yes."

It's Aaschjan—that's an Arcturian ship, couldn't you guess? There are many Arcturians on that ship. Do you want to know the name of my ship?

"Yes."

Mohanya. Now there is a Mohanda, that is not the same, this is Mohanya.

Nice, gentle, caring name, probably a female name. It's probably my compatriot that gave it that name.

Now, let me see. We are come to learn, it is true, but not so much to observe.

There is so much to be with you. To be with humans we can realize that we are that which is maternal, though we are very much like humans and that we have organization and that we have precision, integration . . . soul, spirit, physical integration.

"I have not the most slight shadow of a doubt of any of that. I absolutely know that is true. The arrogance of thinking that this human form was the only Light form—I have never been able to understand that."

It is fear of an attitude because the memory banks are ripped out. There is so much fear here. How could anyone have reassurance here without becoming out of the sky.

"And yet, the movie ET where the being looks similar to that generated more love among the people than anything ever had prior to that, so there is a deep, deep subconscious knowing that it exists."

Yes, they are remembering. It is a very fine attunement they are going through.

"Yes."

So, in my realm it is thinking that has brought us across the wavelength. In your realm it tends to be still physical.

"Umm humm.

There is come a time when we shall ask you to re-signal, because we have made this interaction and made this commitment in our timing. It is not anything you have said before that we would promise to know. It just is. So we be asking now if this is coefficient with you.

"If I can bring it through, I am more than willing."

All right, now in this comradeship that you share with this being, you have said you shall be more still upon your way and spend time alone. I shall be available to make contact with you on this that you call a typewriter.

"OK."

I will not be typing the words. Perhaps you will, but I will think to your brain. Then it will seem as though there is a stimulation process that will come out as though you were not typing it, but you will be, because we will be working the electrical system. Do you understand that?

"Yes."

You are very familiar with this, I believe, from your Arcturian background and you can check with Ashtar. As this passes through your form, there may sometimes be a slight adjustment like this. It is not harmful to you. It is a radiance. It is not electricity like you know electricity. Your availability will assure that we shall make progress. Some times you have been distressed because you have been stretching out too far as you say. Then we can begin, but there is a reason for this, not just teaching.

It is important that I convey my feelings as bastion Commander of all the Beings who are in my corps. They elected me to do this. Who knows why? Probably because I was willing. Humm. But that is enough reason because every one is capable and I like this being a little bit more gregarious than some. I should like to share that which is known as us, and I should like to do this with you if you would like to receive this to be. I think it would be an advantage.

"Oh, definitely."

I know someone who you know who could draw my Beings if you should like to add to the material. The Being is called Jonathan in your language. He has been visiting us. He is a fine being. I like him very much. So if you feel comfortable at some point, he can very swiftly show you what we are like.

"Yes, I met him the other day."

He is nice. He is a nice Being. So, at that time, any of my fellows who would choose to relay messages to you can do that. I shall be primarily responsible because I shall assure that they are smooth flowing. I will not allow a lot of . . . let's see . . . ummm . . . . I can't find the word . . . substitutes.

"Are you telling me that you want Earth Beings to know of you and that if there is a way that we can publish something . . ."

Anyway that you can do this, it doesn't matter. Don't care if it is published or just given out. It just depends on how it is most efficient. My purpose is friendship. I think that, in the long run, the thing that will make the difference to people on this planet is friendship. They seek that between themselves. It is an extended vision that they might seek it among the stars. When friendship is established, then fear can go away.

"Umm humm."

And then the cooperation can come. We offer only friendship. We could offer more, but we are not going to because we feel that what we grow is needed upon our plane and we don't think you would like it anyway. We feel our technology is efficient for us, but it is not what humans might want. We can take them for rides. We don't want to. We are very willing to extend friendship and lots of it.

"Wonderful."

Yes, I think it is, too. We can see upon our screens that which is Earth when we choose to but we do not try, and we do not wish to see very much. It doesn't take long to see what is available here. There is a great deal of beauty. There is a great deal of good cheer. There is a great feeling of longing. We don't need to watch people. We do come and go, so if you have time, we shall come into position. It's easier to work when we are closer.

"Is there a particular type of coding I need to go through in order to reach you? Or, do you just want me to get centered, sit, and you will come? Can I just think to you?"

Yes. And I think you will feel me here, tis not in the third eye, more up here (points to higher on the forehead). That is because of the way my brain is created and it will be telepathic projection for me.

"Umm humm."

And I am sure that will strike you very similarly because the brains are similar but I have more mass because we do more.

"Umm humm."

And later humans brains, a similar structure, will open up more but your heads won't need to grow. That's not necessary. You just use all you've got. It's a different cellular structure.

So, let me see, my old wise one said before we left (he is like your wise ones). He is a fine Being. We laugh a great deal. He's gotten to a point where his long yellow legs wobble together. He talks in an old shaky voice. He said, "Tell me what they say because I want to know before I go if we are going to be friends, or not, and then I can decide if I like them, or not." I assume that means that if humans say they don't want to be friends, he'll decide he doesn't like them. I think he has earned that.

"I think there are many thousands here who would want to be your friend now, but there is still so much of those elements still on Earth, anger and violence, but none of us participate in that. There are enough of us who have a great longing to know more and to associate more . . . and these young ones like she worked with last night . . . the whole group . . . there are so many who want to know so much. There is no problem with being friends. The problem is in getting people and getting the understanding out."

Well, that's what we are about because I know the publishing industry will go through a minor hysteria when it finds it doesn't have enough to feed the public, and then all of a sudden, you will all have this material.

"My only concern is that I have been told so many times I could write these things and I never get it through, although I have noticed that I am intuitively getting much, much more lately."

Yes, you are. Yes, you are. And you will. You have already taken a great deal of material and you have typed it. I know that you can. Where it withdraws is when you go through distress and that makes the airwaves busy, so if you just come with the peace that this space affords, you will begin to move into that next channel. It is a different vibration.

"Do you have any . . . can you see what you feel I will be doing when I leave this job I am doing now? What do you see me doing? Do you see me moving around a great deal?"

Umm humm. Umm humm. I see you teaching, and eventually I see you teaching the Beings about space, and I see you teaching the Beings about being Beings.

"Yes."

Just as you have designed.

"But it begins with something that I can get money from which is probably more concrete in the beginning."

Yes. I see you being available to teach. This is what I see. So, I think that this is sufficient. I think I have done everything I need to do, and . . .

"I'm trying to free myself from that other work so that I have more time and energy to do these things.

Umm humm. Umm humm. When we begin the transactions, let us begin very simply with some introduction at least, and at some point in time getting at what we might call dialogue that can be converted to print, or whatever you want, I don't care. Then we will begin to make it more orderly. First we will check, and get used to each other and then we will begin to put it into sequence . . . the offering.

"Umm humm."

It is important to bridge the gap between nationalities whether they are of your plane or many planes. This is happening upon this planet. It is being brought forth—the gift.

"Umm humm."

What I may offer is the gift of Light because all Beings who operate from fear have no sense of their total Beingness. When they begin to sense that, they completely surround like a flower. They come.

"Oh, there he is. He found his way out."

A moth. That is very nice. Do you have them here before?

"They live only at night. They are attracted to the Light. They are a beautiful being, but they eat our clothes."

Oh my.

"Do you have anything like that on your planet . . . any bugs or small animals?"

We have a small creature like you call a mouse and one like a termite. We have one somewhat like that that helps with the recycling of the food supply.

"He helps to eat the things that you need to get rid of?"

Umm humm. And he helps to turn the garden up. Oh, I know . . . he is bigger like a rodent, like a mole . . .

"Yes. He plows the soil."

Yes.

"Earthworms do that here."

Yes, we have some similar to that, but they look more like your snakes.

(Joyce shakes her head.)

You don't like them.

"No."

That's all right. You would like ours.

"Umm humm. Yours are friendly (chuckles)!"

Yes, I like them because they have some differences because we all look kind of alike. It's always nice when we have visitors and we can look at something different than ourselves (laughs). Sometimes we think we look at yellow faces for six weeks, or whatever . . . this is your time . . . and we think we are going to go next door and look at a different color, or whatever.

"The planets . . . one was blue and one was rose. Are the people on the blue planet, blue? Or are they yellow, also?"

They are blue, (chuckles) isn't that something?

"And you have a sun? Something that brings warmth like our sun? And is it a different color?"

We have seven suns . . .

"Seven suns!"

Interspersed. They are not hot like yours. They are soft . . . luminous. The heat comes from inside them.

"Have you seen the visionary art that is on this planet? People go into meditation and draw it. Have you seen any of those?"

No, I see it in my head, but not here. I have not seen it.

"Let me show you. It is right here. This is a calendar. We keep track of our time (visionary pictures on the Lazarus calendar)."

Yes. It is wonderful. This is lovely. Umm humm. I can recognize this We don't look like any of these beings. You are saying these are upon other planets?

"We don't know for sure. Someone sees these things in their mind and draws them, so the idea is coming from somewhere. Somewhere there must be a place."

If you tell this one, Jonathan, the place of the three planets and seven suns, he would recognize it in his feeling center, because he has been there, and the suns are equated to that which be shining here in the sky on this place and they to illumine, but they do not heat.

"They do not heat."

And it is a soft light not to burn, and inside is where the heat comes from. Heat comes from inside the planet.

"Do you have night and day or it always light?"

It is essentially night all the time or day all the time and that is in a turning of the location where I live.

"Is your planet round?"

Yes. Very similar.

"And it moves like our planet moves?"

It turns three times in a year. Not like your planet. It's not this orbit thing. It's different. It's like a biological clock.

"How old do your people get before they disintegrate?"

Several thousands—the old ones.

"Umm humm. So your little ones in Earth years would be how old?"

Several years, she says. Then they start to stretch and then they move very fast. I adore them, but they wear me out sometimes. Maybe because I started late in life.

"Yes."

I am 2000 your time.

"I would not have enjoyed them at age 2000. And, it was very hard work. I am very grateful for them. They are my best friends. They are also old space souls. They know it, too."

Yes, they are. Well, I best be getting along. I have been here a long time now.

"Yes. It's so nice to have you come."

I want to thank you for this convenience and this conveyance and your efficiency.

"And give my greetings to your wife and to the old one. I hope he will live long enough to see friendship."

I shall. Shall I send him the telephoto of you as I see you? I can do that.

"Yes."

We do not do this without permission because it is considered private.

"You may do that."

You look how you look. He is not on the ship. He is relaying all of this.

"Tell him that someday I will become open enough to see him, also. I am really honored."

I thank you so very much. In our friendship we shall proceed with all of the things we have discussed and I am sure we will find new things to discuss. There is much to share.

"Good."

It is not, in spite of the lack of violence, a boring society.

"Well, let's get me open enough to receive and then whatever it is you want the world to know here, we will do."

If you feel there is a very long shaft of Light coming down through the center of your being, it is the communication system of my plane and if it is uncomfortable, please say so."

"Is it like an obelisk? Is it golden Light?"

Yes.

"I have felt it already."

All right, so it may not be difficult. Your mind is open, time is available and you will be unstressed. Stress causes blockages.

Her body is saying it is hungry. That is because it takes a lot of energy to do this.

"Yes. It is very comforting. It is beautiful to watch your aura."

Well, it is the same also for me. It is very efficient because we have shared so concurrently.

"What color do you see around my aura?"

I see much green about you. You are a very fine Being and I thank you so much for your presence, and now I much bid you 'Adieu'.

"Be in good stead".

Joyce to channel—That was the most beautiful energy you can imagine. You know what it is like when a child paints the sun . . . .

Chapter 10

Hilarion and Ashtar

June 22, 1989

For these purposes, I shall be known as Hilarion. Although you are aware from the many levels of existence, that I can be at any of those at any point in time for any purpose. Here you shall know me as I am, the one Being with Truth.

Now, I have out of the ethers the configuration of an opal ball, this one will look to you as smoky. It is different than you might think. It is opal, it is living flame. 'Tis fulmion (?). I want to give it to you, I want you to hold it throughout this time. I want you to place it where you will. When it is time to write, I shall tell you. The reason I am giving it to you is to enhance your powers. (He asks me to lay this etheric ball in my lap and hold it.)

"Thank you".

It is not to be put into yourself. It is to be put in a place where you can admire it as it grows. It shall lead you to those purposes that you so desire.

It has within it contained the secret of life as you know it on this plane and beyond. Hummm. There is much more here to know. The future brings the destiny of human kind close to that which they originally attempted to create, but by the experience of human kind, we come so much closer to knowing that which we truly are and that which we can truly be, and without this experience would not have done the things that we shall do.

"I see".

This shall guide you upon secret pathways—it is not an initiation, do not think so. It is a beginning. Initiation is provided by yourself. Should you choose, you shall move up rapidly. This Beingness of this stone is allowing you to begin to see what the purpose of human kind is. The secret is the purpose. Without the experience gained by every level, every association, every actualization no matter how disastrous it may seem, we come into this position of knowing. Without this, we are broadcasting our seeds without water.

So we know these things. Experience tells us much of it so we have this then the future to ascribe to. When it has been expanded, this place and the way therein, there shall begin the accumulation of knowledge for the 13th and based upon what we have learned then, the 13th shall become more whole as a design.

When we designed Earth, we didn't know very much. It was a long time ago. We had learned from other places and other times and other ways many of which you sense, feel and know, but nothing so complex as this great and beautiful and strident humanity. So, we come now before the Boards, the governing Boards, that which at every level have watched life evolve. If a being think that there is Source, that is Creator, that is called God, that is only one Being, they are wrong. It is all Beings. But when that voice speaks, it is the wisdom of all beings no matter what they have been doing. But, in the process of creation, we have noted that if the dynamic of Love is pursued, is observed, is honored that the force of Creation becomes growth. If the dynamic of Love is denied, growth stops.

"Yes."

It is not the cause at any level in any sense to stop growth. So love persists and that is a human term. This has within it Life and Light that you will see. It will be in your dreams. It is a gift, not a charge. Do not take too much responsibility here.

So, you have then the 13th Universe. We are amassing information. One may wonder why another Universe. Well, the other twelve have worked so successfully that the next part is, "Well, let's design one from all of the other information." And, of course, you know by now . . . a lot of it is experiment.

"Um humm."

This healing process is an experiment.

"Um humm."

It is an experience, it is a mission, it is anything you want to call it, but, don't call it off, because without this, without you and the others, without we, it would cease. All things—growth would cease—and, now, we feel the time has come to begin what we would call the great push forward. So that can be for some an antagonism and others, not at all . . . a useful experience, a propellent, and as one might feel that they might move on a stream—and another pushed—none shall feel held back. Some shall feel thrust this way and that. That is their own stubborn desire to remain as is.

"Yes."

And that is their way. If I told you that my singular purpose is to design as well as possible, this totality that we are coming to, this 13th Universe, you might wonder why I am present now speaking to you, but I have done this before, this designing, and you were well represented many times and well, well aware of the catastrophes that might occur on this plane with the continued use of free will.

"Yes."

I thought it only fair that we might discuss the possibility of extending into the 13th this use of free will, but retaining the dynamic inherent that you call Love, the force of creation. The only way that can be done is by literally visibly raising the current if a society is off beat.

"Yes."

That reminds them they cannot see, any purposeful and reasonable reason in allowing this to occur again.

"I don't either. It has gotten way out of balance. There has to be a way to keep it more in balance without allowing it to go so far into the violence, to the anger . . . but the free will is a wonderful idea, the choice. That is where growth is—the choice. If we are truly to be co-creators, then free will is imperative. But, there has to be some way that this doesn't happen again, or it should not be left to go so long before we turn it back, or something."

A signal.

"It is far, too far away from the Light."

A signal so that when that begins to occur—the tipping of the scales—that is it. There is a balance in all things. When you look at Nature on this plane in its freedom, there will be times when something occurs wild and ghastly, but soon the new shoots come, but it is swift—years, not milleniums.

"Yes."

So, it is a signal so that when the balance is tipped, it can be corrected before . . .

"Yes."

. . . it turns itself upside down.

"This is what is so difficult for us now. If we were just pulling up, if we were just writing the effects of this lifetime, it wouldn't be nearly as painful as pulling up eons of time trying to bring up all of the programming and change it. That's where it gets into really a difficult situation, because as you change one little thing, it triggers changes everywhere. It's like pulling on this elastic mud that . . ."

That pulls you back.

"Right, but the free will is a *marvelous* idea."

Within strong beings . . .

"Right."

of rightful purpose . . .

"Yes, of clear Intent. As long as we could keep the focus on Love and Peace and Joy instead of anger and ego and running wild with emotions—if there were a better balance—maybe by taking, by transmuting somehow some of this energy . . . most of this energy . . . getting rid of that so that we went on from a higher vibration, as you said, with more thoughts of peace, it would create an incredible Universe."

Sooner. It would allow these frequencies of free will to ascend with the evolution of the species, but, if it began to tip, to signal sooner not to allow just attempts, but absoluteness.

There is gravity here that is intensely . . .

"Yes."

. . . powerful that pulls you down, in fact it is at points destructive.

"Yes. Umm humm."

If you defy that, each being of this natural element knows what happens. Something like that—a natural law that says this is not the ordained path of growth.

You see, it is so incredible. Free will exists without the Universe. Every entity has free will, but when they are close to the Source, they cannot deny and their growth is based upon the acknowledgement of the process of creation. This Love dynamic is so interesting because in humans it has been created as a functional apparatus . . . expression . . . but that's not what it is. It is creation in motion.

You can have such complete love, it would seem to have no emotional impact at all and it is creation in motion. It is total detachment. If then, that law is denied, defiled, that is the secret. That's it. That's it. There is a point in time when that law is denied and that's not workable material, so it has to do with the signal that the balance is tipped. It is not any more viable creation. That's it. Yes, I shall speak about this to Commander Ashtar. This is very good.

Now, we have a signal for you. Ashtar wishes to relay through this instrument, I, that you will be correlating some information about how these disasters can be avoided in the future. It shall come upon the typing and you shall know what it is when it comes. This will be simple for you to receive, this information.

"OK. I hope so." (chuckles)

It will because you will be given the time . . .

"All right."

. . . and you are already in the force field. The information shall be kept in a separate folder if you do that. It is not to be shared except with those who *really* understand and you can determine *who can hear.*

"Yes, I understand that point very well."

All right.

Ashtar—Haelegram, please be aware that the actual hologram is a distended or extended version of that which is Truth because what it does is display across space that which is time and Light. When you put the particles of information into the Source vibration called creation and extend that through the proper avenues, they can reassemble in another space. They are being fed, originating, but actually creating from here to here.

You, in a sense, are a hologram because you have your native intelligence still upon your planet and ship. Do you understand and feel this? You are fed from a distance with a portion of yourself. Now, you can begin to draw on that. Not to bring this all into this. We have already discussed with you prior to this time that it shall become that these portions of yourself shall integrate.

"Yes."

It shall be as I have just described by the effective method called a hologram, for here exists your source vibration, the Creator. It gathers impetus, your Being, and it becomes erect on the planet called Arcturus. It then gathers impetus and goes to the ship and gathers again and goes to you. This doesn't mean you are less.

"I understand."

It means you are more, and it means that at each place you are gathering data. You are coordinating events to assist this one. All of that is centered within this other awareness consciousness which is your total Self. That is what allows all of this to take place. It can be understood through understanding Universes and dimensions. Universes are places, dimensions are vibrations. This Creator is creation. There isn't anything anywhere else. It is us . . . and you know this. It is this that somehow the people must begin to understand. They cannot feel this immediately. They will be very frightened.

"Yes."

But they can later. They can pretend that there still is someone else somewhere else, but sooner or later in order for creation to be formed, they must comprehend, they must take that advantage to themselves. Then, they truly become responsible. It is a significant change in vibration. It is simultaneous. The unknowing and the knowing are one. And these unknowings suddenly rise to the point of being knowing. It is so close and yet so far because it is vibrational. It is dimensions away from them.

Is your ball growing?

"Yes."

Interesting, it must be collecting information. As then, you become very, very aware how compounded this information is for you and you allow it to go to those who can absorb it and use it, as you become aware as a teacher of how you must scale this information down, it is still the primary purpose of all that we do to acquaint each one with that which is the highest and best of themselves. What they do with that is their purpose.

In the long run, the scientists, the technologists will endorse and embrace this factualization that each being is *the* creator, *the* creation, as co-creators then. Symbolically, people will begin to stand together, because whether they stand together or not, they still must face that within themselves, there is that which is the Oneness. There isn't any place else. They can stand apart and it still is, but they must stand together.

If you will take an event, it will begin to be a feeling of much more scientific for you. That is only because it is *literally* an expansion of energy and it has been measured in your society scientifically. Allow this to be measured in your feeling. You are as sensitive an instrument as any Geiger counter, as any seismograph. You can understand and feel what is happening. It doesn't matter where. Trust yourself. More and more is there. You are a very effective instrument for your own purpose. Trust exactly how you are feeling and let it float there. Don't even analyze it. Let it just float there. The answer will come.

As your Self is divided into portions, so shall your attention occasionally be divided into portions and you shall come to understand more and more because the attention will be coming from here or here or here. And you will submerge as one because you are the Oneness as then this stronger purpose speaks for you, through you. You become Creation in motion on this planet, and you are getting samples day after day how that works.

Soon, you will not be astonished. You will be your primary nature instead of your secondary nature and then you are an example for how that works. That is how it will happen. And observation will teach these Beings why these Beings seem to feel comfortable all the time.

You have the sensation of too much to do. That will change, and you will be given a way in which there is not too much to do for there is sufficient time to balance your energy and your cash and to be able to do what you need to do and have the play time.

"That would be nice."

This will change. It is in motion beginning very soon to express itself. So, do not be surprised if you are moved away from the lodging before October.

"That's fine."

October now is the thinking stage.

"And the work will still be through the teaching? I can teach much through real estate classes."

Well, there will be more beyond that.

"One of the key things that we could really benefit from here on Terra is if we could teach integrity and ethics in business. The way it works in the big world is not the way I ran my office. It's not the way I trained people. It's been a real learning experience for me, but I needed to learn it. I needed to see how it is done. The key word is still nurturing and there is no nurturing."

So, in this focus, we have opened up the plan which you have suspected.

"Yes, I am ready."

And . . . it is in the works. When the works begin to work, it is quite amazing what can be seen as part of creation. In this plan, there is this which is the novitiate coming to the teacher and the opening is made, and how you weave it is up to you.. You have been designed flawlessly. Do not ever suspect that you do not know what to do, because if you hesitate, and you feel you do not have the answer, just let it come in. It is very much available. The only way it cannot come in is when it is blocked. You are seeing many examples of how this works for you and others.

So then, it is true, it is an apparatus that we are preparing for you that allows you to teach ethics in business, but that is a portion, and after a while, you will have trained others to do that, because that is fairly simple once you catch on to the ethics. What you are able to do beyond that is far more. And essentially, you will be training groups of people to teach the populus, and that is later. So we are in the base, as you have desired and designed and it is like this.

So the momentum is picking up for the first part of the plan, and you will note that there are many of your particular wave who are going through these same things . . . new beginnings very much in evidence.

"Yes."

New beginnings may sound redundant, but that is the fact because they have never been seen. Never on this planet have these things been seen. They are new beginnings.

Now, we have testimony for you to lift the ball up very high above your head and close your eyes, if you choose, and feel the weight. Feel how it really is and to sense its beauty and durability and to know it so well that it becomes as an object of your dimension. I shall be still here and let you experience this. When you have felt the full impact of the ball, bring it back down to your lap. You do not need to hold it in the air. It has a truth lodged in the center. It is for you, not another . . . and it has this which is the coded message of your individuality which it shall bring as a flickering Light. It shall help you to open that which is the realm beyond that you desire to be with. As you know that can change in size. The ball is fundamentally Truth and it contains the seed of the secret.

When you have this availability as you have chosen to express in the Cosmos and you choose to be in a society as you have, we can tell you that as this concludes, if you choose, you may take on an assignment with the 13th. It is a rare occasion to be given that honor and you have not already designed that in your note path, but after this, we feel you may want to take a vacation.

"Not a very long one. I get bored. There has been much good in all of this. Much joy, many deep relationships. It's been good. It's only painful at times."

Now, more about the note path. We should like you to begin to take in the sense that you have been seen to do, what do I call it . . .

"The writing."

Well, there is another word—shorthand. We know that you have the ability to understand the symbols. We want you to begin to draw something. Do you have a pen?

These are my directions to you. Attempt to draw, although this will be a little hard to do from the top left to the bottom corner of the page a straight line. (He goes on to have me draw a crude star and have me divide it into parts—this is very rudimentary because I am not an artist!)

This then represents seven dimensions in five spacial units. We are not even talking twelve—five being a smaller sense. As then, this is a Universe, it is divided logistically and it goes on and on and on. It is not round. It is not horizontal or vertical. It just is, and within this complexity, there exists one place in time where galactic energy will be available to allow this to begin. The seed.

"Um humm".

From the seed, there begins to expand, and this begins soon, because this timing already is lifting. As Terra has been oppressed, as a human being that has been oppressed starts to stand and stretch, so this is beginning and out and out and out it goes and in a precise position in the center of this vast complex structure within structures and times within spaces and dimensional variations, there exists a precise, very precise positioning. So, this is just an example to try to show you how this may seem to some incoherent and to others very exact.

"Um humm."

The way that it is exact is by feeling sense how it pulses, where the seed belongs, what vibrational tones say this is the exact space for this to grow and in other senses, looking at it, it seems to make nothing, absolutely nothing will grow here, but it has become.

This new life pulse was first generated in the co-creative balance creation by those who were insistent on raising the vibrational of this plane so that it could live again. If it had been sealed, it never would have become . . .

"Um humm."

. . . so this place, this seed contains the fertility of that moment, not a wanton moment, a feeling one, and the giving, the gift as all we give you grows and grows and Life begins—all representative of the beginning times for that place.

What that seed will do is make a space. There is nothing in that space yet. There is no child within that world. It is only a beginning, so our work still is concentrated on this plane to expand it to the point of allowing this space. Then, when that space comes, these configurations change, their possibilities change, their distances change, and always it remains that if any time in this one can feel their way to position, feel their way home, know the absolute that says, "This that I feel is creation because this is the dynamic that I have known so well." When one tempers with that dynamic to an extreme, it comes over here and things happen.

"Yes."

In this process, there is that which is a built in theodigm—you know this word by now. It carries its own thoughts already, so it is not like a seed that cannot grow. It is indeed a living seed.

"But the seed has been impregnated with Love, Joy, Gratitude . . ."

Yes.

". . . caring, tenderness, rather than all of the opposites,"

Yes.

"so that is what is going to be the beginning seed of the 13th Universe."

Yes. As it is then, now a thought process, it is in place being that process. It is not now even a magnetic force. It is a Beingness, do you understand that? It is not a physical mass, it is a beginning.

Actually, if you looked at it you would see that it seems to be a hole in space and time, and it is the void, and it exists there because the transfer of energy that was all of you chose to come to this place and give of your gifts, brought that possibility from the void. The void contains everything. It is a place, the way, but from it must come all that can be created. Then, by that feeling sense of all of you, there began to be this new place, this new way to expand like this and any who choose can manifest the creation of that into viability, but the criteria is that it follows the dynamic, the principle.

"Yes."

That is why we invite you to consider being in position to assist and that dynamic will require an effervescent body not be burdened with flesh at that point because it is fast, flashy and movement in order to really confirm properly.

"Well, as they say on Earth, isn't that where all the action is going to be?"

It is so. Indeed. Indeed.

"It would be very exciting."

And it is the first time we have done it all. The rest have been done in stages and we know so much and we can take all of this that we learned here and make many planets and many beautiful cities and it can be a small Universe or a large, it doesn't matter. We think, perhaps, we would like to make it a small one at first and experience it getting back and forth and then add to it. Do you think that's a good idea?

"I think it is always better to start small and have it be pure essence rather than diluted . . ."

Yes . . . pure essence. There are some places that are like that, but they are old. This is new, but experienced. It is like your master souls that come to hear you speak. They are new, but experienced in how this will be.

"Aren't they wonderful, my children, the young ones (speaking about a high school class she teaches)?"

Yes, they are.

"What a joy that has been! That has balanced a lot of stuff to have been allowed to be a part of their lives."

Yes. I can see why. Marvelous experience! So, being a hologram is not so fearful, is it?

"No."

It merely is a movement of energy through time and space. Molecular extension is a hologram. It is exciting in the society, but it is new for the scientists to discover, but really it isn't anything new, and they are very happy that finally they have seen it. It has always been present. The hologram is what will allow the latent images to come into being . . . the latent images those things that are flora, fauna, minerals. It is what is happening with your stones and as it already exists, it is being projected through time and space.

You have worked with this a great deal. I am probing your memory points. I think I would like you to go from here to Venus because it will soften your Arcturian background and bring forward the scientific, but softer. The hologram for that which is plant life is designed. It is a place, you can see it when you walk in the parks. Do not lament those things that change because there is something coming in its place. There are lessons to be learned upon the journey.

The hologram for humans isn't coming. Yours came with you, but it can always be expanded on. The hologram for animals is being designed. Minerals . . . that is interesting. There is more flashing out of the minerals than anything else on this plane because they go everywhere. It is strange they become part of all living things. When the soil has disintegrated—stone—they become part of all living things.

"And the new ones are so much more colorful and beautiful. They are really gorgeous."

Stones are the living cells contained within the soils of Terra. It is to those you look for many of your answers. Feel them and pull them to yourselves.

They can tell you the secrets across time and space from the void that exists beyond God. There is coming that which is the future.

So, if in this Universe you can sense the latent image and sometimes see it, and you feel good and trust that, that feeling releases that which is any other dimensional evaluation. It means truly there is no concern because it is there shimmering and all of this must go on its way, and sometimes when something is going, it is very hectic.

Be very aware that you, yourself, can create just by being comfortable with what exists, and as the latent image shimmers higher and higher and you feel it and see it, that is confirmation that the old ways will be let go of so that the new ways are in position or absorbed and expanded. Who knows what might be useful? And those beings who are sending the images creating the pattern for society to dwell within as it grows are assisting you much on this scale because of the imaging field.

You never know where they have implanted; therefore, when the two of you went off to the neighborhood, you might be surprised to look again at another time and see what has been created there. Some neighborhoods like that have very great comfort. Others do not. As you move—feel, and that you did and you were accurate, but another time feel. You may be surprised because the work goes on very rapidly. From this you learn, more and more so that the next time we have a very great application of energy that says now we are going to do this and it is ready for habitation . . . and you know about moving. It's nice when it is ready.

There, I have talked a great deal. I shall listen if you have questions.

"Well, my questions—I don't think it is important for me to understand at this time. My questions still have to do with if time is going on all at the same time—I understand fairly well molecular extension because I think I do it all the time as I surround my children as I do my morning meditations . . . I actually go, I know that. I send. I think that's part of what you are meaning by molecular extension—when I work with the Light and send.

But it is hard for me to understand how time goes on and on and on in a linear fashion and still is all happening at once . . . but I don't think it is necessary to know that right now."

No. Let's touch on the edge of it. Mostly, you have to feel it because you can't bring it into this linear comprehension. You can't.

"I understand how as this expands, this perhaps this one would become thicker and this one might become wider and how energy does all those things. I understand that part."

All right. Let's talk about feeling of time. Let's talk about the sense that you KNOW that you exist here and your children exist someplace else and you can move through time and space, and I mean more than you thinking about them, I mean a portion of you goes.

"Yes."

And then, let's think about you on the ship and that you, indeed, can move through that distance and be there, and let's think about if you wanted to move through dimensions to the Source . . . and you have done this in meditations. You have been there and who knows where that is? Who would describe the journey and how to go there? If you can't feel yourself there, there's no way to go there. You can't go in a spaceship or shuttle or rocket. That is how you really understand what I am talking about.

"So, what you are telling me then is that instead of dealing with linear time, we are simply dealing with feeling time?"

Yes.

"That's very simple."

Very simple. Feeling is intuition. It's all the same thing. It's a sense. You are sensing time. You are sensing time and as you act on that, a bridge is created. There is no gap. It is instantaneous.

"Let's explore for a moment—young Tom who is in the class and his microphone—he speaks to himself on the ship. It's just continual input night and day. It's not only input, but perhaps protection? Is one kind of watching out for the other?"

No . . . one is informing the other . . .

"Informing the other . . ."

but it is going both ways. He doesn't know it. His brain activity is recorded in his brain activity. It is just a simultaneous action. It could be done without this apparatus that you saw, (etherically) but it enhances it, so why not. He doesn't notice it until he is really, really aware of it and then he is masterful and he keeps it. He doesn't fling it away. Humm. So it is utilized. It is the same kind of apparatus that his form wears on the ship. But there he takes it off because he sleeps and walks about and scratches his head. Here he wears it all the time because it is density and he doesn't even know he is wearing it.

"And he has the same female companion both places."

Umm humm.

"But some of us—like I am male on the ship and female here. It doesn't matter, does it?"

Oh no. No, it creates a balance. There is something we wish to discuss and that is you have been given the time and space and confirmations of cash flow so that you will be able to take some time off for yourself and be with the softness now. In this sense, that you came to earth and became business like, that in itself is linear and it sets up a barrier that frustrates you so. Then you put an Arcturian in business and you have a double energy system. What we desire is to let go that barrier regularly so that you can become very soft and *that* allows the flow that you want in order to receive information.

One of the ways is that you have been shown movement and that you like. You can move and that allows it to keep moving out the energy. After a day after you walk, if you can do it before you eat even, or, if not, after—do some of this to stretch your form because it takes out that which is blocked hanging on to you tight and lets the energy move. Then, be with your friends, be alone, do not take on any more classes.

I wish to address the one called Bernice. She is a fine being, very highly evolved and does not, in this sense, conform into her energy how she is. She does not understand. She is coming into a new trial in which she will be assimilating a great deal of energy. The feet will swell like balloons. She won't ask you for awhile. She won't be about. Then she will and then you will show her and it will be dramatic. We want you to set it up as a way that you would work together, and when she mentions payment, allow this please, and see it as a confirmation. It can be donation type that allows her more leeway.

First, work with the feet and colors will flow through you. You need not think anything. This is full range healing competency. You will be able to take out the poison and the lesions and the things that trouble her. It will happen so swiftly, almost overnight, and in a week, she will be walking again. But then she will have seen the sign that says that you can confirm for her the things she wants to know. Then a very subtle sequence will start by you teaching her some things, not all classes, but some things. In this sense again, you can trust yourself. You will know exactly what to say and how and it may end up being just friendship sessions and we see them as not drawn out, but very simple and samples to her of what she really is. Her feet will be the example. She is creating this. I am not. Her Self doesn't understand it, and that is why her feet are swelling.

"Is she going to work through this in that marriage?"

This is an example of trust, these two together. They don't know how to squabble enough to clear the air. They don't know how to conclude the marriage. They don't divine that they even have to, but they don't have a very great comfort level. It is coming soon to decide one way or the other. It doesn't matter to me. It doesn't matter to us. He is a nice Being.

"Yes."

If he opens up a little, once he does, he can completely support her, because he doesn't mind if she knows and does these things. He just doesn't know because she doesn't know, so it really doesn't matter either way. But she must decide for herself how to become whole. They are too interdependent. They are doing different things for dependency sake. Very possibly we would help some. It is a good sign when Beings can continue to work together.

So I think we have done what we needed to do. Do you have more questions?

"Not really. It has been quite a mouthful for me to absorb."

Umm humm. Don't be afraid to start the typing next week. It won't harm you at all to spend a little time. You will be quite surprised what happens. Another thing we are working on is stabilizing your income force so you don't have to spend such a length of time.

"Great! The yellow beings the other night were great. I will enjoy working with them."

They like you a lot. They are learning, too. It is important for them to be able to spread their cheer. They have the inability to be sad. They have the inability to be angry, mean, show rancor. They can show disturbance, but is more . . . they are so dear, it is more like a muddled shuffling about because their energy system is disturbed and they have to all think about it.

They are vast this realm of beings. I have watched them from afar many times and I have come to visit them many times upon their great ship, and I want you to see them sometime in your mind for they are quite large and you would think them to be cumbersome, but they are not. They would be here, but they shuffle. It delights me. They blink at each other and talk about things in very whispered, excited tones. That is the most you will ever see. It is kind of, "What shall we do about this?" So, when they come to you and you may sense that regularly, if you say something that startles them, you may feel this little bit of shuffling and blinking. Then when you explain to them, you feel this—"Oh", this sigh of satisfaction that this comprehension has come. Hummm.

So, you will have this through the relationship with them as they grow. I find it very delightful and when they encounter anything that is an obstacle, they don't stop and think twice, they go right around it . . .

"Humm."

. . . and if it is a Being that is stubborn, they don't even deal with it. They just don't consider it valid. They just go on their way. That doesn't confuse them. They don't shuffle about. It is very clear to them. It is very clear to them that this Being needs to be left alone, so . . . they do. And if you ever watch them as they come into an area where a Being is troubled, they automatically part and keep going. The Being is just standing there and often it is one of themselves. It is not ostracism. It is only that this Being vibratorily states that he is not in compatibility with the group and we will just keep going. Even if it is their mother-in-law or they came to dinner.

Very different society from here. No heavy obligations that say you *must* do this. Like, "Oh no, we don't do that here." You felt that when they said that they did not feel that they had to feed this planet.

195

"Right, right. That was marvelous."

And, they don't even want you on the spaceship. You wouldn't fit. They have a different design in their dwelling space than humans require.

"What does the vibrating wheel around their ship do?"

It is a directional. If you do this, you go this way.

"And the power for their ship is like liquid crystalline."

It is fluid . . . uum humm. Very pretty. It is like that. It sparkles, but it is fluid . . . flow.

"And it has a great deal of intelligence, the fluid?"

Yes, it is part of the planet. The planet is living, like Terra, but many do not know it. Many, many planets are living, vital organisms and the people merely request what they need.

"Are the Sasquatch, the Bigfoot going to be instrumental in bringing in the technology in a few years here?"

Yes. Yes, and then there is a refinement process beyond that. There is no limit to this. They will bring in a particular stage and that will alleviate some of the distresses. Their beams assist the technology to come through and then beyond that, there is more refinement.

"If there is any forest left for them to hide in—the loggers are busy."

There is a point when they are through. They are here to a certain point and then they can go. It is up to them. We will take them on the vessels and take them to the various homes that they have chosen. They know all about this.

Now, that thought applies to what I stated that you never know what is coming and you cannot lament what is going. The great whales are considering if they should continue to live as a species. The porpoise will stay, very dogmatic little creatures. They wanted to do this. They desire. Bear, the great bear may go. We shall see. But, all of that says, in its time, that is all right.

Many things have lived here and gone home—Neanderthal men—a subspecies, not your beginnings as human race, a species that came to test the waters . . . see what it's like . . . existed in co-patterns with other more refined beings. All of these things will be available in the sense of the *feelings* because the information that comes for the brain is so staggering. Already, much is come and people are blinking, "Well, we have no record . . ." Well, that's all right. Here's one.

So, all this takes a while to sift, and shift, and fit into position and some of it will be very amusing to watch, some not at all and that's all OK. I know this is a challenge. We are all asked to become 4th dimensional beings—actually 7th dimensional beings because 4th is not equipped for the work. We will be standing about wondering why in the world you ended up just as you did tonight in the neighborhood and in the place. Why did you end up here, because you are not vibrating at that rate? But there are other places you can go.

"They give us a choice."

Exactly.

"They let us see that that is not where we wanted to go."

And there are other places very similar where you can go, you see, where it is comfortable. Don't think you are being locked away. You are provided an example.

Now, I must go. I have been gone a long time.

"Yes, thank you so much for coming."

It is my pleasure. It is my welcoming format to your new intelligence, your new work. Huh! This is the end of a cycle and the beginning . . .

"Yes."

. . . many, many are experiencing this.

"The sadness has gone away. The frustration is not nearly as much as it was before the seminar on Saturday."

That is excellent.

"For me to see that it is the end of a cycle, for me to see that part of it is the pain of the earth, for me to see that it is not my personal thing was very important and I can let it go."

That's right. When one thinks it is their own, they tend to keep it.

Well, we have much to discuss at other times and we shall do so. Many times you will sense there are things we want to tell you. It's alright just to doodle and let strange patterns emerge. When you begin the typing, the first energy system will not be exaggerated. You won't feel anything that is untowards—unusual. The miracle of this is that as you adapt and adjust to the flow, we can increase the frequency, so that it is easier and easier to assimilate and the information comes faster. If you will look back to where you were receiving information and then the change, you will correlate that there was an energy shift in your living pattern, and you couldn't receive us easily.

When it is time to shift into a soft, high vibration, then as you are existing in that, living in that, Constance can help develop that. (Constance is my house angel) We have done a lot of work this week with this Being and the others to assist in expanding the energy field. You won't have to do much at all. It is fine. This energy, then, of you, vibrating at a softer, higher rate allows us to even faster expand the field and then it will come swiftly. And then you can sit down and in one half hour take something and you won't have to make all these big shifts because you will stay.

Our best and highest to you.

"Thank you so much."

Ashtar leaves, Hilarion is back—We would appreciate that you wouldn't converse much about the 13th, but feel that you can, if it feels appropriate.

"OK."

And any time that you wish to design or think or discuss, we can play this game.

"Ok."

Just for fun. Not for, how shall we say, actual serious working—that is too much of a burden. I don't like that. I like to go fast and swift and take some time off. Well, my time is over. Thank you.

"Thank you for the energy."

Oh, you are welcome.

At the time of this channeling in 1989, I had no knowledge of who Hilarion was; however, as I came into the knowledge of the book, <u>The Seven Sacred Flames</u>, I discovered that Hilarion is the Cohan of the Fifth Ray, the green ray, a magnificent ascended being who works with Raphael and Mother Mary. His retreat is The Temple of Truth in Crete, Greece. He was a great healer during his life in Palestine (290-371 AD) and he performed many healing miracles and made his ascension at the end of that life.

"He was also able to heal with the touch of a hand or the command: *Be thou made whole.* He walked in the shadow of his 'I AM Presence,' being humble before God and his fellowmen. He gave God the glory for the miracles of healing performed through him." From <u>The Seven Sacred Flames</u> pg 133.

Sometimes, the enormity of what I received in these transmissions so many years ago is overwhelming! I am so honored and so humbled!

Chapter 11

Zeron and Sananda

March 14, 1988

The channel, Gayl, and I are having a discussion about what our bodies need to handle this energy and to help with the candida that has become a real problem for both of us.

Gayl—The cleansing process that I was in was calculated to relieve a lot of the debris from my system that created differences in my perception and actually created pain in my body. I remember now saying to the Guides, "Couldn't we just localize all this stuff and pull it out?" and here it came all over my face. There were a lot of ways that dovetailed and gave me a lot of messages, but it did this huge detox.

I had already started using liquid chlorophyll. Have you used that?

Joyce—"No."

Get it at the whole food stores. Get small bottles. What I got has mint and alfafa in it. It's a detox thing. It's not horrible. If you overdo it, your kidneys hurt, because it is really cleaning. Another thing to watch is your lymph system and for that I got fenugreek and comfrey—it's from Nature's Way—it's call Fenucomp and it is for the lymph.

Joyce—"The candida affects the immune system."

Just go to the store and get the bottle and hold it against your body and you will feel that you will either surge forward or step back. Often I will get 'Oh, yes,' or 'No'. Sometimes, it will do 'Just let us think about this,' but you will definitely get your own reading. Again, watch the chlorophyll, because as mild as it seems, it really cleans and can be really stressful. What I do is take a glass bottle and put the water in it and pour in what I think—I just let my body do it. But if I, intellectually, think that I will speed this up, my kidneys will hurt, and my back hurt for about two days before I figured that out.

So, this is part of your process right now. I am getting like a scan. The scan is saying if you don't move fast you are going to have a glandular disorder which is going to be stressful. I think what you want to do is both a characteristic cleansing—OK, they are saying, "A facial cleansing with Light. Allow it to seep deep into the nodules and the surface of the skin." What I am seeing is White Light, but you will know what you need to do—and then also, a detox program with—they are saying, "Fenugreek Comfrey does not feed the cells quite so well as Liquid Green, also called Barley Green."

Joyce—"I have seen that."

Barley Green, I think goes through distributors and is expensive. In the health food stores, they have what is called Green Magma. Barley Green is dried and is very high protein—the chlorophyll and lots and lots of enzymes. You see it is sprouted and growing like wheat grass, but wheat grass is too intense. You can put the liquid chlorophyll in water and drink the water, but Barley Green tastes different from that. What people have found is V-8 works really well—not fruit juice because that clashes, but V-8 works well. It is like 80% protein and it rebuilds the cells. This is really important to us now. I suppose you would refrigerate it after you use it.

Joyce—"How much do you use at a time?"

What I am picking up for you is a teaspoon in a glass of V-8 juice, in a tumbler that you can shake. They are saying, "Drink two or three times a day this Barley Green. Allow yourself to get used to the transition and then increase or reduce the dosage accordingly as you need to. You will know. Your body will gravitate to it." Chlorophyll first, then Barley Green . . . that gives you time to plan in your budget.

My daughter and I have been doing this and what we are finding is that it works really, really well. Some days you don't want that chlorophyll and another day you will need a lot of salad and your body will say, "Do this now," but the point is eventually to work with the Barley Green as a staple part of the diet. It means we are rebuilding the cells at a cellular level getting the Light through the cells and the protein balance which is so important. I have been struggling with that.

Joyce—"I know. I am, too."

I feel better when I eat meat, but I don't digest it, so it's like later I feel better, but then I am getting all this junk in my system and I really don't want to do that. I would rather switch into . . . they are telling me sprouted grains. In your stock, your hand will reach for what you need.

I have been into colors, so Basmati rice which is white and broccoli which is green is like I am amazed to eat things that taste good. Browns are out. Yellow, white, green, not red, not purple. The body will choose from whole foods what will sustain itself.

But, back to sprouted grains, if you know from the body that you need a certain thing six to eight hours later, then you rinse it and put it back in the water and let it sit there and be softening. Then you bring it up really slowly, so instead of boiling water as the instructions say, you soak it, and it starts to soften, and when you bring it up it sprouts. You will see in your grain this teeny white tail right at the end of the grain. There is rolled oats, rolled barley, and rolled rye that you can sprout. And then all the other grains, the wheatberries and the rye groats and the barley—there is no hulless barley—basmati rice and oats—not so much corn, but some.

Joyce—"That's another of my allergies—corn."

OK. Corn is harder to sprout because the kernels are so big. But all things that are grains are ground to flours. If they remain grains and then they are sprouted, they are seeds. So the primary foods are seeds, protein, minerals, oils. So instead of oils in the salads, we have oils in the seeds. I have not had good luck sprouting sunflower or sesame seeds. They get really bitter, but there are other ways like toasted sesame and kelp. That is what I feel for you. It is not a macro diet. It is different. That is where the Barley Green comes in because the protein content builds the cells and everything is protein and water.

Joyce—"I seem to crave protein ever since this hypoglycemic thing a couple of years ago. I am trying so hard not to eat meat and things I can't digest."

Custard and goat's milk work for me. Green Magma is not quite as balanced. You will have to track down Barley Green through distributors. So any way, this is really important. It is part of the thing I have described for you and I was supposed to tell you about it.

Joyce—"Yes, I have been getting swelling in my face and hands again. I don't know if the candida is coming back, but I don't think it is."

I think you are on to something with the edema and pressure points.

(Arcturians come through with the following):

'Cellular structure in the mid-terminal mind is being revitalized. Do not allow yourself to wonder too much what is going on. You will know this when you come into the forefront of the activity. Soon, the play is about to start. And the timing with the precision application of energy, the substance of the form called cellular rehabilitation/revitalization is about to begin. Do not allow this to be critically acclaiming your attention, but be aware.'

Joyce—"Well, I hope something is about to begin. I have gained eight pounds and two suit sizes!"

'The timing for the intercellular resurrection is about due. Don't be surprised if the surface starts to peal just a little bit—the skin. Don't be too surprised if when the action of the energy comes, it will be as if you were struck by a lightning bolt just a little bit, but benign. You know those jolts that you get. Don't be too surprised that if you lie down to rest, you will almost be pealing off a suit of armor—the same thing we have been talking about—a shell. It sounds more prevalent like coming closer.

Don't be alarmed by allowing yourself to imagine that anything coming along is wrong. You don't have time or justification for that. Don't be in that process. Don't allow the modes of injury to come into you, for those are the crevices through which the sustenance of dark service do creep—a crack in the armor. Don't let anything come to you which says that you are justified in having uncorrelating energy. There is just no truth in this. Don't be in any way but the greatest and grandest gift of disguise.

Don't be laughing at the wrong things, but laugh very much. If in your wisdom, you can calculate that now you don't have to serve so well because now you can lie about and relax—perhaps this is a grand gift after all.'

Oh, they are saying that if you are not feeling well to go lie down. They think it is a great joke. There are some who need to do that. Some are super serious and they wear me out. OK, this is something you will go through and learn about, and it is something you will transfer to the people. So, the other part is to bring the vibrations together and this is in the visioning process. You can ask the healers. You always have to ask for their help. As the bodies are going through these processes—and you know more about the bodies than I do because I don't work in those terms. I was sitting in the doctor's office waiting for him and I got that the subtle body is rising faster than the other bodies and now I am getting something about the causal body. See I don't know these.

Joyce—"The subtle body is a term used by the Sikhs."

It has to do with the seven bodies and I don't work with that, but it has to do with the different parts not what sets up as an abrasion, so what we have to do is go past all the parts and say, "I AM this Light", whatever Light comes to you. I am told to use this Light and let your hands do the symbols. It will come and it will all just happen, so you don't have to go to somebody. Ok. That's all.

Sananda wanted to talk to you.

Joyce—"The energy is huge."

I am not Sananda.

"Who are you?"

I am Zeron.

"Oh, you are?"

I want to tell you a few things and then we are going to do an experiment.

"All right."

First, I am not your Commander, I know that. I know evidences, though, that you don't know yet, so I am going to take an active lead if this is convenient for you. This is not an order. This is in a format of being presented. When I present things, I have a certain habit with novitiates, so you will forgive me if I seem to forget that you are an advanced comrade and I am coming much as in advisory capacity, but still I am used to taking command because I have had to do that. I must do that much. We will lead forward for you and we will complete the training very fast and for this moment of energy, I must take a correlation. Then it will be done. Then we can cease.

When you presume to know much, and you do, when you know, you know much, then you can have this Commander's position. It is yours, but you must accord to that excuse attached to that. I know you are not attached, but approached. When that time comes, you will know, I will know, everyone will know. You will have a grand ceremony. You will be just in that position. Now, don't endeavor to know very much at all because we will be giving you so much information you won't be able to catalog it, remembering, but just stored. You know the brain cells have portions that are unused.

"Yes."

Those cells are being opened by this visitation. They are being opened visibly and you could record that. These cells contain the management incorporation of a star fest. You have that memory tract. You have been accorded into a management position again.

As Commander—in—Chief you have, at times, served under a celestial vessel that houses the brain and body of the great Sananda. You have these memory tracts. You will remember visits with Sananda. Now, Sananda, when he comes to Earth is far removed from one . . . gallant that I know upon the vessels. He is much ascribed to. He Knows things. He knows as much as I do and many times more. He is not circumscribed. He is not cut away. He is not made different. He is always available. He has this habit of being disarmingly versatile, absolutely accurate all at the same time. I tell you this in advance in case you don't remember.

When Sananda moves into position, it is a juxtaposition, and brings everything else into position. Mere movement of the mandate, the Son, causes things to happen. This one, whom I adore, is coming to visit you soon, tonight to speak, but soon. A body you will recognize and the room of your home when you are alone is overcome. Don't perceive anything, just be aware. You do not see. Don't worry. You will see soon after. You will know.

So . . . when the Sun moves, the heavens remain, and the resounding sound is the symphony of all time. When the Son steps into position, many things are created. Some have come into the presence, but somehow have not recognized. They have thought this to be a simple fellow. They are disarmed readily, and by their own innocence, they are dismissed.

So, I tell you these things. It is not often that one is visited by Sananda in these realms at all. For now, the purpose is to discuss what you would rather do next, not tonight, but in the service. So, I will let you discuss that with Sananda, and during that time, when you are concluded, I will visit your body and you can perceive that you and I will visit with Sananda and she (the channel) and we will experiment.

We are opening the field. That is why this is necessary and you have no qualms, so we will move extremely fast. Do not think that this is normal. Most do not do this. (Laughs). It is not for correlation only; it is for fun, too. It is good to have fun. I like to have fun. I am laughing a lot now. So, I will comment no further. Do you have any questions?

"I am just hoping that after this interaction tonight we will be able to work without having all of these people."

Yes. Yes. That is multipurpose, as you can imagine. It is to gain admittance. It is to strengthen your field. It is to allow the other people to participate. It is very important that people be drawn together. You need each other. When too much comes to soon too easy, it is easy to closet it, and some have kept away the truths. You know this by being a part. It is not important to be a part. It is important to be available to do this. So . . . that is all for now. Do you have any questions?

"The visualization that I got of the grid—I believe that is what is was— some thing that felt like metal—my position on the grid in this area is along the coast, is that not correct?"

Yes.

"And what I got from that is that I am like a transformer no matter where I walk, it just keeps going. Is that correct?"

Yes, you are like a sphere of Light, a transformer (laughs). Yes.

"This (gestures to etheric headgear) is very interesting."

Yes, it is quite grand.

"I have all this figured out. I haven't got the rest of it."

This is very attractive. (Laughs)

Oh, yes, it is very nice on you. Wait until the rest of it comes. Your suit is available when you are ready . . . and you should see the shoes. They have wings on the side of them. That was your addition. That was humor from an Arcturian . . . winged feet.

"Well, we need all the Light we can get!" (Laughs)

This was the humor—with the speed of Light I go. Some have adapted to this. Now, it is perfunctory to see that you will be getting in touch with me soon at your own motivation. At that time, we will move much faster.

"Do I need the sign on, sign off thing? Can't I just bring down the Light?"

Yes. Yes, and any time that you like, call my name and I am there.

"Is your color energy like a blue gray?"

Yes. What do you think yours is?

"I don't know. Aleckatron keeps talking about pink, but I don't think it is pink. Blue green is what I feel comfortable with."

Yours is almost like a gray green. It has the slight greenish tint. If you saw the suit that you wear, it is a combination of threads. You know this. You have it on Earth. It changes and it is some blue and some green. It is very beautiful and it fits you very comfortably. Each ship has its insignia—very nice almost a flower design. Do you see it? Take a good look at your symbol. Continuous protection. What else would a communicator be but continuous protection for others.

Ok, I go so he may come.

"I am very glad to be doing this."

I am, too.

"Hope we can get this armor off."

Have to go.

I am Sananda.

"Hello, Sananda!"

Welcome to this time.

"I am glad to be here."

I am very glad to be here.

When your Truth arises from your mark completely, you will not need this shell that you created when you first came. Your space is being devised and you know this. Things are being given and you know this. All things come in due process and you know this. All of this time you have been waiting. Do your think you have been waiting for nothing? You have been waiting for the ride home. When the moment arises, it will divide the shell and the moment can arise at a moment's notice and you won't even have to ask. It is you beaming your thoughts and your heart as one that will give you the key.

There is a cycle of energy that moves between this space and this space and you know why an Arcturian would have to involve this space with this space . . . because it is practical. You can see much further, right?

"And more directly."

Yes. Now, this is a revolving energy, not as a wheel nor as a sphere. It is outwards and back and outwards and back. It is slow because you do not want to be disoriented, but is constant. You can go to that space. You will revitalize your memory. You can sit with it and know this action. The Light that it inhabits is the golden and white combination. These two spheres come together twice around your clock and the action correlates the clock of the zone that you live in. That is just a convenience. This is what can separate the shell. You will not need that action anymore, ever.

So, for this time now, we are going to work with Zeron so that you have a complete compatible arrangement. We do ask that you arrange yourself comfortably, and as the action of the Light is so much incorporated into your work (is that comfortable?), allow us both to do the Light again and allow this one to merge and allow the body to relax. Be aware you will not be left out. Allow this one to completely immobilize the personality of the body. It is why I am here. It is safe. That is better. You can have more room.

Now, Zeron is very large and you have a small form. It doesn't matter. He won't stick out. All right. Let yourself become that what he is. Let yourself begin to sense that which is beyond the means of Earth. Let yourself be as the vessel for all time merging. Let Zeron have the ability to speak. There is nothing barring that transmission. You will also be speaking, Joyce, but it will be more difficult. It will be more the sense of hearing yourself speak. You may do whatever is most necessary.

I am Zeron. I am glad to be here.

Sananda—She is a very apt pupil. I know this one you speak through. I know her well. I love her. Since we have both been upon the vessel together and have gone many ways together. I do perceive that she is very valuable in communication with many people.

Zeron—I perceive that she does this in a very common way. She is a good communicator. She also has healing ability and her Intent is so clear that many others see her although she says almost nothing. They get the vibration of the Intent.

Sananda—I also see these.

Zeron—I perceive that she will be a valuable point for the ships to key into. The work will become very intense along the coast.

Sananda—Yes.

Zeron—I feel that I can train her rather quickly. She is willing to do whatever she is asked. It will have a lot to do with communication and the ships. She is a trained teacher and can communicate on a very basic level.

Sananda—Can you tell me what you most perceive as important? What is next in this work? She is telling you in her brain cells what she wants. You can speak to her. You are now blending. She does not get that she has this power. Zeron, open her brain cells and allow her to see that which is hers. In this moment, she can become collated.

Sanada—Do you see, my friend, Joyce, the energy that is being released and the spiral light that is encompassing? You are being transformed to a posture of your awareness.

Joyce—"I can certainly feel it. I can certainly feel the part of the brain where it is being opened."

Sananda—Now you sense your power. You are part of you, part of Zeron. Compiled into your one brain cell is the recorded data of your sojourn upon the planet Uranus where you did study with one called Jillica. This will be brought forward so you can teach. It will be a comprising of energy providing Jillica comes and speaks through you.

Uranus is the holder, the keeper of many of the secrets of mankind. It's so interesting that they (Earth scientists) sometimes think Uranus not compatible. It's a cosmic joke, isn't it? Now coming forth also from Uranus are strains of the melody of the time, the rhapsody of the songs, songs of the people. There is much to tell if your friend, Jillica . . . and now Zeron speaks.

Zeron—She has no fear of your presence here, but you don't have to be so reticent. She cannot know you yet until you tell her how you, what you are. It will not harm her at all, but if you feel your hand upon her heart, know that this time is spent to alleviate further time and questions.

Joyce—"Is the work upon my ears so that I can hear better, is that what this is. I have no trouble feeling any of that. I have trouble getting the thought past."

Sananda—It's all right.

Joyce—"There is a great deal of activity around my glands, my pituitary—"

Sananda—Yes. We are passing through time. We are hurrying the processes.

Joyce—"It is all very joyous."

Sananda—Zeron is having a grand time. He is now released. Not with his hands, with his Intent, with the beam from the center eye, he can focus in thought and precision by Intent. Not precision by sight . . . precision by Intent. He is allowing the energy to flow about inside with your brain capacity and open the glandular elements so that the energy may float through. The energy is opening the intercellular process. It is done very swiftly almost as you might suspect laser surgery. He is a very accomplished artist, a musician this Zeron. He enjoys playing in this way. It is in sound and color. Some of what you hear in your ears is sound, but not picked up appropriately by the human beings. You will rise to that sound, too.

Joyce—The colors are amethyst and blue.

Sananda—Yes. You are making much progress because you have passed through the dimension of time. Are you comfortable? You will begin to hear strains of music. There is a spiral of Light going down through your body. You are feeling the energy system that is your portion of being part of the grid. You may see a spiral. It is being centered and located on the grid. You may go anywhere on it.

Now we are going to reverse the spiral. You will feel a corresponding rising energy. It is your complication, anticipation or correlation issue and from it meets and spreads and broadens the space upon the people. The need of the organs of the body to adjust is necessary. You do not want to overdo these energies in the beginning. Do not ask for the energies to be pronounced at this time. Let them become at their own will. They are intelligent. Those on the ship will not activate the new systems until you are ready. We don't want you to receive too much. The body is not quite ready. The cells have to be activated. In this way, they are being raised.

Joyce—"So much is going on in my ears and in the front and center of my head."

Sananda—The strains are very, very light. Try to adjust it, but let it be as part of your understanding.

Joyce—"I see the color, but I can't bring the music in."

Sananda—That's all right. You will get it. You will see it pulsing back to you. It is given you directly by Zeron. Now they are opening more of the access route. You are receiving a full dose of liquid Light. The magnification is coming forward. They are separating your shell.

Joyce—Amazing!

In a semi-sleep state, Zeron will come and you will see this magnification of energy that you are a part of.

Zeron—It is done. We are finished. She will receive more information in her sleep.

Joyce—My head feels very heavy right now.

(Much of this tape was very quiet and impossible to hear. Discussion was between Sananda and Zeron that he, Zeron, did not need to be so serious. He could lighten up. This was fun for them to do together. They bid farewell and said they would see each other on the ships.)

Sananda—Are you back? Are you feeling OK? I am very proud of you. You have accomplished much.

Joyce—"Yes, I just feel heavy. I hope this process goes quickly and I get to where I can communicate."

Sananda—See how you stopped yourself. You are exactly where you are supposed to be. How do you think you got to where you are? And everything before. Be in peace in your spaces.

Channel and Joyce discuss what has happened. Gayl speaks—This energy in this room is so powerful. I could barely see. I could see your eyes. It's like a time warp that dissolves the molecules and everything is moving energy instead of static energy and then it almost all blends, except it shakes.

That was really interesting to me because this is the way I want to work. It is what I have been waiting for. It is not like Ramtha who comes on full bore for those people that need to be there. This has been the process of people moving through the energies. When he said the things he was going to do, I could see the changes—intensity—most of all I could feel the spiral coming down. It was like one coming down and another going up at the same time. They went together somehow and passed, you know how energy can do this and this one went through those rings.

Joyce—The energy in the glands in the center of the head was really something.

Yes, I could sense it.

Joyce—And whatever they were doing to my ears—it felt like they were pulling them down. I could *feel* music going across. I couldn't hear it. I could see the color and I could feel it.

Channel—One of the things we worked with this weekend, but I have just really been learning about, is that we can become our Source frequency by toning to become that frequency and we can do it by toning, by humming. Your body will just naturally go to a level, a tone and it may start really low and move up and it may move up and down a few times. My voice has a certain range and sometimes I can't get up there, so I get as close as I can and then you can just hear it, but that toning comes also with a Light color, a frequency color. That frequency moves you into your starlight position and then you become that. That's where you can manifest from. Nothing can penetrate.

It's like an instant meditation that can keep going and going all day. They said let's not use the word 'dark forces'. Let's use the correct word. Let's use evil. God is creation, creation is growth, growth is live, opposite of evil, not die. The opposite of that, of course, doesn't work and it comes back in and whatever it looks like will end up back in. It is reassimilated and reissued.

Sananda has a school and it is very close to Source. That is where the energy goes to be recycled. It is called the School for the Integration of the Heart of the Inner Self. I am sure it is a tone.

I like people to really understand because people freak. You know about the Earth. This immediate layer is the evil. It is not working. It is sticky. The next layer is the populous and they really interact. These layers are always getting stuck. The next ring or sphere is the awakening, the seeking, the enlightening all mixed up together. Then there is another ring that is the enlightened ones, ones who came from the hierarchy to teach and speak and all the ones like us, and then it just keeps going back to God.

So, all of this process means that we manifest from a level of vibration that we live at—our tone takes us to this outer ring and maintains a constant so that when people are down here freaking, we don't have to get stuck, but what happens to me is that when I get overtired and vulnerable and in some way get enough of me down there, I get stuck and then pull myself back up . . . climbing back up. For me, I am still letting go, letting go, letting go. I don't have to get stuck in the enlightening ring. I have done that, and I think most of us are that way. Some are supposed to work in this area.

What they did with you is set the tones. It's clear light like crystal, the cut crystal, or a nice stream, and I have been feeling that for years and years, especially when it is by a clear stream. It's like I dissolve. Very pleasant. I found out that by getting into my frequency, then you don't have to even think about the beams coming down or breathing of the Light, it's like you become this total energy system and you are part of the Source again. You are not even on the earth. You are back at headquarters and you just have this access in all directions.

I found out you can use it. For instance, in another town, I had a young woman come up, first time and there she was, and she had a lot of healing work to get done. She came up afterwards and said, "I need some energy." My old reaction was, "So do I," (laughs) but I know now you can pull your invisible act. It's like you can just see yourself as this Source energy and give her all she needs.

That has been just a tremendous liftoff point for me and I have found that I am getting to that point with people, no matter who they are—I deal with it with my children, my husband, my Mom, with my friends—it's like what you are doing is your business. Go—I love you, I support you. If you want advice, ask me, but I also need to let you go. What you do with the information is your business. It's like, "Just do it."

I know I have absorbed a tremendous amount of guff from people. It's like "Just give it to me and I'll take care of it," and we get to do that anyway for the Cosmos. We don't need to take that on.

So, that is the whole process we were doing tonight—opening the energy system. I saw it happening. What was really interesting was when Zeron was widening your magnetic field so the magnetic resonance was not just a single line of energy. It's a total system, the whole Cosmos. It's like your etheric body was Universal instead of just going to here. All of these Rays, these antennas were going everywhere. You just are the Source. I saw it and I sensed it. It was just going right out through this room. You . . . you were the center of the energy.

(Immediately after this session, I began using Super Blue Green Algae from Upper Klamath Lake in Oregon, a wild natural product that I have been eating for the past 23 years. I give it so much credit for my perfect health. It rebuilds the body from the inside out when taken properly.)

Chapter 12

Arcturus and Captain Haelegram
On the Fleet Communications Starship—
Simulation Data Center "AASCHJAN"

The following information about Joyce (Captain Haelegram) was received and channeled by Johnathan Hammer on September 22, 1989. Johnathan lived at that time in Salem, Oregon, and was able to go in through the eyes and do drawings of the over soul. A copy of Johnathan's drawing which has been framed and hanging on the wall of my home for the past 23 years is included at the end of this channelling. Johnathan told me that he sat opposite this Being on the ship and that Haelegram was a formidable Being. This is the best and most detailed information I have ever encountered about my home planet and I have been most grateful to Johnathan all of these years for providing me with this touchstone of my homeland.

"I found that the information concerning this received transmission-visual very interesting and most assuredly astounding. The Aaschjan is the Star Class Fleet Vessel from Arcturus and is capable of housing 12,000 inhabitants comfortably. Its population consists of 59% Arcturians and the rest of other nearby associated planets and moon systems. The ship consists mostly of what we would call living super computers and serves all of the

Ashtar Command Fleet Actions, wherever they may be. It is also a central communications link to the star systems in all twelve Universal Realms and all dimensions in those realms.

The Aaschjan is one of twenty five such crafts in the Ashtar Fleet, but it is certainly the largest. It is considered one of the greatest vessels of the Arcturian Fleet of ships, and it returns to its home city port on Arcturus once every 178 years approximately. Its city port, the main space fleet center, on Arcturus, is called Hathspuuud-Rossmathyste (translation: Greetings in Love to All—the City of the Mother Life). It has a population of over 25 million, 15 million from the planet Arcturus itself.

This great city is the third largest on Arcturus, and serves as a port city to a great many vessels which land in the great desert of Anthripidiaes. This city is a cultural exchange center as well as a place of business and exchange where documentations are created and received from the galactic tribunals. These documentations usually concern the growing and exchanging of crystalline power sources and food supplies, of which Arcturus is greatly famous in the fleets for providing. You can see the different crystalline plains about the port city, parcels of blue, yellow, red, violet, indigo and emerald. These crystals are grown and harvested to be transported to other worlds or to be delivered to spacecraft, or to be utilized in the manufacturing of materials, tools and art works.

The great desert of Arcturus consists of silicate sands, amethyst dust, rose quartz particulates, citrine, onyx and hematites. This is the area where craft great and small may land. The desert of Arcturus is not a natural formation. These specialized sands were imported from the planet Xeoanan, located in the third Universe, 8th dimension. It allows craft to land upon the desert without the usage of flame or thrust. It acts very much like a conscious tractor-beam.

This city port surrounds the core-length to the center of the planet. This area produces the purest and richest forms of rose quartz and is so high in frequency, that it is what lights up the Arcturian atmosphere at evening and casts a glow out into space. The Arcturian sun is very far away, but the atmosphere is charged greatly with rose quartz particulates that capture the sun's light and magnify it. Although the sun is far away from the planet, it is very warm there, reaching minimum temperatures of 85 degrees. Most of this heat is caused by the 236 moons that orbit the planet, so the heat that is experienced is electromagnetic, not environmental.

Of the 236 moons, 189 are habitable by Arcturians, and 52 of these are habitable by humans. These moons are areas of industry for the services that Arcturus provides. There are also sanctuary moons for rest, relaxation, recreation and even sustenance, for there are 12 moons consisting entirely of rose quartz energies. The largest moon, Haamadgathene, is pictured to the right and is a spiritual moon where many may go for sabbaticals, ceremony and vaulting. Vaulting is when an individual goes into deep hibernation in a place where he/she is sealed from the outside environments.

This is a very peaceful and tranquil place and no craft may land there, but it can be reached thru teleportation systems located within each of the three great cities. This moon is capable of sustaining all life forms in all universes and all dimensions and provides a constant and spectacular view of the Arcturian planet.

The mountains are lightly dusted with snow quartz, and Arcturus even has a polar region, although it is not very cold, only 78 degrees. It has mountainous terrain, high cliff areas, deserts, plains, and dense tropical forest. There is a wide variety of animal life, and a total of 9 races upon the planet.

The area of space surrounding the planet is filled with rose and amethyst quartz particulates that are the remnants of an ancient moon-planet that nearly collided with Arcturus eons ago. The water that is upon the planet is a viscous fluid that is almost completely transparent. It is issued forth from springs in the mountains and also from core deposits of the primary home stone, rose quartz. This fluid is essential in the growing and harvesting of all products upon the planet and is also an essential to the life forms of the planet. (To have a taste of home, take 1 cup of Karo syrup, ½ cup of water, 1 tsp. mint extract, pinch of salt, 1 TBS of heavy cream, 1 tsp of "live" yogurt, and a pinch of nutmeg. You may want to add a smidge of blue food coloring for effect.)

The floors of the ship are plated with rose quartz of varying frequencies and colorations. Most of the individuals prefer to walk about with bare feet or wear very thin soles of kavlakthis, a rich leafy plant that is much like the consistency of leather when dried and "tanned". All illumination panels are created from crystalline structures, and you will be interested to know that there is a very small amount of mechanized structure on this starship.

The Being, Haelegram, is standing in front of a view screen of woven clear quartz and silver threads. It is powered by the thoughts of the individual and is set into visual structure by the glowing frame of topaz and citrine silicates woven with gold threads and clear quartz rutile.

The structure to the left, with the many colored balls of energy is a musical instrument. One simply tones, and the color structures change and shift in frequency, or, if you have no vocal capabilities, you may "touch' the energy globes with the hands or another appendage for the same effect. One can conduct a symphony with such an instrument, for both the hands and the voice can be utilized. The longer one touches the spheres, the greater the tone, and the faster one strokes the sphere, the greater the pitch and color of that frequency. The colored ecliptics at the base of the instrument store the sequence of what is played and can replay the created music at a later date should one wish to listen and not play.

The smaller structure near the middle and at the bottom of the page is an art form as well. It is created out of special metals and crystals that one or two can manipulate frequencies and color effects by utilizing a control panel. This too has a sound to it. It will hold the image until it is reprogrammed to create another, and it will also store that which is created for later display. Both instruments of creativity respond to the frequencies of thought as well.

The Being, Haelegram, was at one time, a crystalline Arcturian. The Arcturians wished to establish a kind of center on the continent of Atlantis at the beginning of its technological era, and sent many representatives. One of these was Haelegram. This one allowed his Arcturian form to dissipate (die), and ventured to Atlantis where he was born into the form of a female and served as a priestess of crystalline technologies. After many years, the manipulation of the crystalline power was being developed and abused, Haelegram left Atlantis on an Arcturian vessel to return home, not wanting to be a part in the destruction that he knew would be catastrophic. He took with him many technologies and instrumentations, leaving the Atlantian scientists to stir their own technological pot.

On returning to Arcturus, Haelegram, being a male entity, found himself in a female body and wished to become male once again, but was accustomed to, and enjoyed the human form that he had, so set himself into a course of events and transitional healings to set the frequency of the form into a more crystalline structure, allowing the masculine frequency of the self to shape the body at will.

You are here for a great many reasons, one being to experience the human female form once again before the masculine body of the Arcturian-Terran form becomes complete. What is wished here is to retain the feminine frequency in the soul pattern to return it to the Arcturian formulation so that once the transitional form is completed, Haelegram will be a masculine entity with the balancing of feminine vibration, adding a subtlety to the consciousness and bringing it into closer consciousness with the Arcturian Planetal Goddess. It is also hoped that you shall be here to be integrated as Atlantis begins to rise from the Atlantic, for you have many keys and formulations to the unlocking of a new nation.

Upon the starcraft, you are considered one of the highest qualified for the position that you hold and are usually quite busy in the communications center of the craft. You are also in direct communication with several of the other fleet commanders, who with you, monitor the changes in the crystalline grid of the Earth planet.

As an individual who is beginning a second stage of incarnate crystallinity, you are able to assist both physically and telepathically/empathically in the healing of these structures as well as with physical crystalline beings.

There is much blessing and love sent to you and many support your work here. This information was received from many comrades and Haelegram as well, upon the starship Aaschjan.

Received and channeled by Johnathan September 22, 1989

Continued the following day . . .

Haelegram wears s semi-transparent gown of a crystalline material that is translucent in the colors of green and blue. It has weight to it and flows almost like a liquid metal. The belting is metal and stone and carries a piece of the pure rose quartz in its center. When there is a need for such sustenance, one simply strokes it with the fingertips. The other stones surrounding it are of a similar nature but for different purposes. Attached to the headpiece and the waist belt is something similar to a conductive harness. It is very strong and yet very flexible. It is composed of crystalline and metallic substances reorganized into a molecular matrix that in essence creates a new and unique substance.

The head piece is comprised of over 168 different crystalline structures and mechanized devices that enables the wearer to have direct communication to the data centers and the supercomputers of the vessel. There is also the ability to link into the computers of other vessels and, indeed, even those upon the Earth, which at a later date will be essential.

The hair is very much like conductive glass filaments and at times will radiate and shimmer with light impulses and become very sparkling. Some of these main fibers, which are indeed very thick can be set into a placement that is very much like linking directly into the main computer entries and accesses.

The headpiece is activated by thought waves, and the hair will respond to this as well as it will show when Haelegram is pleased and joyous, relaxing, very busy, or is feeling displeasure. The body of Haelegram is humanoid with the illumination of crystallinity caused by the Arcturian transformation. The coloration of the lips and eyes is a natural cause, and will lighten as the transformation continues. Haelegram's body is very lithe and smooth, but also very muscular and powerful. Haelegram wears his Celestial Symbol at the throat piece of his "harness".

""There is to be of the coming times that we shall be in closer communion as we have come to be with these actions upon the planet Earth and there are a great many things to be done. As You, this portion of my Beingness, begins that which we shall term, the third stage of Crystalline evolution, which will come in the times of your next Spring and Summer. You shall be in the knowingness of that which is the completeness of why you have come to exist separate from the whole of your totality. This incarnation upon the Earth planet that we have taken, is a highly respected event, for it was not necessary that it be done in this fashion, but as we have done in the past, we shall do now, for we are whole-heartedly committed to this action here. I shall begin soon to be more in attendance of your actions and I shall be in greater communications with thee.

I AM Haelegram, most beloved of your Beingness and most dedicated to that which you are choosing to fulfill upon this place. I love you greatly, and I AM only a step behind. Follow the greatness of your love and serve the Father-Mother Creator that is within, and you shall be with us soon, once again.

You are in the presence of the Divinity of Yourself.

Be it so in Action.

I Salute you, And I anoint you with the Waters of the Mother Goddess of Home.

Vresshammaahd."""

Received and channeled by Johnathan
September 23, 1989

Chapter 13

The Ashtar Command

More than twenty five years ago, I happened onto books channeled by Tuella about the Ashtar Command. They are some of the only books that I finished and then immediately started again on page one. The binders of these books are broken, the pages are falling out. I remember sobbing all the way through the one entitled: Project: World Evacuation when the plan by the Command at that time was to completely evacuate us should there be a nuclear attack or should it appear that the planet would flip on its axis. At that time, each of us had spaces on the millions of ships where we would have been housed and fed for as long as there was a need . . . and they would have come in and picked us up! I was touched beyond belief that we were so cared about.

Every 25 years, this planet is measured (by the ships, I am sure) to calculate the amount of love over fear and hatred on the planet, and the first time that love tipped the balance was in 1987 after the Harmonic Convergence when so many people migrated to the energy vortexes on the planet to pour out love that finally it was determined by Heaven that we were worth saving and maybe as a planet we could "make it" to ascension. I remember the news articles about the strange people collecting on the mountains doing meditations and rituals and how weird we all were.

My friend, Tennie Bottomly, and I stayed at Paradise Lodge and sat on the side of Mt. Ranier reading the Ashtar books to each other during those two days. We saw each Light Worker that we knew in their place of residence on the planet as a gold Light in the dark night and we stated their names out loud and connected the dots with streams of gold Light not knowing until much later that the work we had done along with thousands of others had tipped the balance and created the opening whereby Kryon and 100,000 of his etheric beings came in 1990 and changed the magnetic grids around the planet, an enormous job that finished at the end of the year 2000. Since then, a third set of grids (the first being gravity), the crystalline grid system around the planet, has also been completed.

It was because of the Love energy of the Light Workers that this process was allowed, and this created the opening that allowed for so much energy to be streamed onto the earth at various times during those years, especially at the stargates of 1/1/2001, 2/2/2002, 3/3/2003 etc. It was not that the magnetic grids were completed and then it was determined that there was more love on the planet than hate; it was the other way around. Because we had raised our vibration enough that there was more love than hate on the planet, it was determined that the planet would not be abandoned and everything possible would be done to bring in the energy and the focus of heaven itself to allow ascension to happen. Prior to that time, it was thought that the planet would have to be abandoned and we would have to be evacuated.

When the continents of Lemuria and Atlantis destroyed each other with nuclear energy and sank, remnants of those advanced civilizations who survived found their way into the center of the Earth so that now over 5.3 million people live in several great cities either along the sides of the interior of the Earth in cities under Mt. Shasta and Mt. Lassen or in the hollow part of the Earth with great cities under Brazil, the Himalayas, under India, the border of Mongolia and China, or under the Aegean Sea to name a few. With the destruction of their continents, these ones determined that war had absolutely no purpose and if they were going to evolve, they would need to position themselves somewhere where the surface storms and the energies of war could not keep them from their growth.

If you consider the numbers of people living presently and having lived for thousands of years inside the planet, and that many of us are living multiple lives at the same time either in other star systems or planets or in parallel lives in places similar to this, you can begin to fathom the tragedy of what would happen to those souls if the planet was destroyed by nuclear energy. We came so close to that happening in the years of the Cold War and in those years when there was underground testing of nuclear devices.

In February of 1947, when Admiral Richard E Byrd flew through an opening leading inside the Earth, he found not ice and snow, but land areas consisting of mountains, forests, green vegetation, lakes and rivers and was met with advanced Beings who had a sobering message for him to deliver to the Surface World. He was told that he had been summoned there because of the atomic bombs over Hiroshima and Nagasaki, Japan. The following information is taken from Byrd's diary, <u>A Flight to the Land Beyond the North Pole</u>: <u>The Missing Diary of Admiral Richard E. Byrd.</u>

He was told by the ancient Master who met with him that in 1945 and afterward, they tried to contact our race, but their efforts were met with hostility. He said that the recent war was only a prelude of what was yet to come for our race and that it would rage on until "every flower of our culture was trampled and all human things leveled in vast chaos". He said that perhaps by then we would have learned the futility of war and our race would begin anew. This was the message they wanted brought to our government.

Of course, when Byrd came back to Washington in March of 1947, he was interviewed intently by top security forces and a medical team, branded as a lunatic and kept drugged and locked in an asylum in the interest of national security. Finally, after 64 years his secret log and diary are available.

The twin flame of Ashtar, Commander Ashtar-Athena SherAn is currently serving upon Earth. The following has been taken from her writing, "The Ashtar Galactic Command", pgs 193-196, <u>Messages from the Hollow Earth</u> Channeled by Dianne Robbins, copyright 2003, 2011.

"The Ashtar Command is the airborne division of the Great Brother/ Sisterhood of Light, under the administrative direction of Commander Ashtar and the Spiritual guidance and directorship of Lord Sananda Kumara known to Earth as Jesus Christ our Commander-in-Chief. We are also known as the Galactic Command, the Solar Cross Fleets and the Orion Jerusalem Command. We are the Hosts of Heaven who serve the Christ, our Most Radiant One, in His mission of Universal love. We can best be understood as celestial or angelic in nature, functioning as councils of Light upon missions of Holy endeavor in accordance with the Divine plan.

As a member of the Galactic Confederation, we oversee this sector of the Milky Way Galaxy protecting the Divine plan against any type of interference or violation of Confederation Law or Melchizedek protocol. We are here to assist humanity through the current dimensional shifting in consciousness, the transformation of your physical forms into a less densified etheric-physical form capable of ascending with the Earth into the fifth dimension. We also work in coordination with our brothers and sisters in Telos and their Earth based Silver Fleets under Commander Anton and with the Melchizedek High Priest of Telos—Adama. We are all working together under the authority of the Office of the Christ, the Great Central Sun Hierarchy (Throne of God), and the Order of Melchizedek. We also have our bases located within mountain ranges, in desert areas, and under the oceans. We, our bases and our Merkabahs (aerial chariots or starships), are invisible unless we wish otherwise. In order to see us your vibration would have to match the wavelength upon which we are manifesting. We, and our higher dimensional vehicles, are composed of etheric matter, as real and solid to us as your environment is to you. Thus we appear by lowering our wavelength to match the third dimensional vibration and we disappear by raising our vibrations beyond your visibility range."

The Ashtar Command is composed of thousands of starships and millions of personnel from many civilizations. Many of them, such as Lady Athena and myself are currently living on Earth and we will return to our respective points of cosmic origin when our service here is complete.

She goes on to say that Ashtar first appeared in our solar system in 1952 in response to urgent messages that Earth was trying to detonate the hydrogen atom, a living organism, an act in violation of the Confederation Law. When he saw the devastation of our ecosystem (which formerly had been known as the Garden of Eden in the Universe) and that we were delving into nuclear fission for defense purposes, he sent delegations from the High Council of the Ashtar Command to meet with our government.

Even though the US government will not recognize them, the Ashtar Command is attempting to neutralize excess radiation within our soil and atmosphere and deflect potentially dangerous asteroids from impacting the planet. They maintain the stability of our axis and do what they can to relieve the stress on the tectonic plates directing earthquake activity away from populated cities. They are universal ambassadors of peace, peacemaker/diplomats, and peacekeepers.

This planet has not been part of the Galactic Federation for eons of time because of our violence, but it is hoped that soon as we rid ourselves of the Illuminati and end wars and violence that we can once again be part of the Galactic Federation of Light. Several ones on the planet have risked their lives to leak information about who and what is controlling this planet and the Command is a prominent player in the disengagment of the strangle hold that has paralyzed us for way too long.

Because we on this planet have been held back for so many years by the Illuminati and those not interested in creating a world that works for all, we are far, far behind our space brothers and sisters in technology, in energy production, in providing food that would be beneficial to our body structures, education, medicine, the media—even the weather is controlled! Illnesses are created, drugs are produced to further suffering, pain and stress, and all of this is done by 1% of the population. 99% of humanity is suffering because of the greed of the 1% who have no right to be here. All of this will change as soon as the Federation is allowed to make contact.

As of this date, it is still too violent here for the Ashtar Command to land, and because they cannot in any way interfere with our free will, we are going to have to make these changes ourselves. Ashtar had hoped that contact could have been made by the end of the year 2011, but plans have changed numerous times since then because the financial systems and the governance systems of the planet are so controlled by those who do not have the best interests of the people at heart.

When St. Germain lived on the planet some 200 years ago, he brought about the idea of compound interest and the gold he placed in banks at that time now supposedly is an amount with 40 zeros behind it—this information came from St. Germain himself in the last couple of months. St. Germain also had a great part in the creation of NESARA, the National Economic Security and Reformation Act, which would have forgiven all world debt, mortgage and credit card debt, abolished the IRS and the Federal Reserve, initiated a new US Treasury Bank System in alignment with Constitutional Law, returned Constitutional Law to all courts and legal matters, released enormous sums of money for humanitarian purposes, and released over 6000 patents of suppressed technologies such as free energy devices, antigravity and sonic healing machines, among other things. It was hoped that could be accomplished by the end of 2011. Hopefully, it will still be forthcoming.

St. Germain was one of the ones who had great input into our original Constitution and Declaration of Independence. In the 1930's, in the first book in the series published by the St. Germain Foundation, Unveiled Mysteries, St. Germain says that for over two hundred thousand years, "The Divine Plan for the future of North America is a condition of intense activity in the greatest peace, beauty, success, prosperity, spiritual illumination, and dominion. She is to carry the Christ Light and BE the Guide for the rest of the earth, because America is to be the heart center of the 'Golden Age' that is now dimly touching our horizon."

Though I have read this book many, many times, there have been many times during the last administrations of our government that I couldn't see this as ever happening, but now the dawn IS on the horizon and the Divine Plan WILL be carried out. Every day there is new evidence that the stranglehold on America is loosening. More and more people world wide are rising up and demanding their freedoms.

1 follow religiously the channelings of Ashtar, Sananda, St. Germain and a group of Arcturians (by the way, the Arcturians will be the ones bringing in the technology; the Pleiadians will be the ones making first contact) through Susan Leland and www.ashtarontheroad.com which originates in Maui. I was there in October for a conference with the Maui Grandmothers called "DeMystifying 2012", probably the most sacred experience of my life.

In August, I had a reading through Susan Leland with Ashtar. For years, I have had contact with Ashtar and kept the insignia of the Command and their mission statement taped to my computer desk.

I AM . . . A Guardian of the Light!
I AM . . . Love In Action Here!
Co-operating
With the
Ashtar
Command

I AM . . . Dedicated to
The Kingdom of God on Earth
Interplanetary Fellowship
and Universal Peace.

As the day came closer for my reading to be done in a phone conversation, I got more and more nervous. It's not like me to be nervous in a situation like this. The person on Earth I would most like to talk to is the Dalai Lama, but I could have talked to President Obama or the Dali Llama and been less nervous than I was becoming. After all, this was my Commander, the only one I considered to be such. I painstakingly wrote out questions I wanted to ask, and then ten minutes before I made the phone call, wadded them up and threw them away.

When Susan came on the phone, I told her of my nervousness. She laughed and said he was easy to talk to, that sometimes he could be gruff and sometimes he laughed a lot. He would talk to me first and I would get over my nervousness. She said the group, the Mentors, were there and excited to talk to me.

Susan went into her meditation and then this booming voice came through.

"Hello there, Commander!"

He called ME Commander—you could have pushed me off my chair with a feather! "You are Commander, You are a Messenger of Truth, You are a Starseed, You are a Master." He was talking to me. I was blown away!

He told me many things. He roared with laughter when I asked if my photos, like the one on the cover were really lenticular clouds that covered the ships (he knew very well that I knew they were). He asked what I knew about Arcturus—did I remember the University, the cultural centers, the technology? He talked about the New Jerusalem, the huge city-ship that is the command center for the Ashtar Command, some 200 miles across, now anchored over Washington, D.C. It is from there that he commands the fleets, and it is there that Sananda, St. Germain, Sekmet, Archangel Michael, the group of Arcturians and the others congregate when they are not off on other business.

He told me to have patience, to be diligent, to persevere and to be the Love that I AM. He said, "All is well in your Divine Kingdom. You are powerful. You are Commander on Earth Mission which becomes even brighter as you go."

And for that reason, I am putting out this information about the Arcturians and the others and their connection with me because I feel it is so important that humanity know their Divine purpose in this time of change.

Several years ago, it came to me very clearly that Ashtar and Archangel Gabriel were the same person, because in the hierarchy, you EARN your position, and many of the great ones have several different "jobs". In the chapter with the kids, Ashtar said that it was one of their jobs to bring the soul that was ready to be birthed on this planet and beam it into the mother's body. Considering all of that, is it any wonder the Star of Bethlehem was so bright for so long? I think Ashtar and the Command brought in the greatest soul that has ever lived on this planet. No wonder the angels sang!

Epilogue

As I was thinking about a way to conclude these writings, I went to a shelf where I have kept things that were important to me in this work, opened a loose leafed binder and the page opened to the following transmission. Even though this was given to me in April of 1990 in an automatic writing, it is absolutely perfect for today. Ask and it shall be given. Truth is never far away.

May the words on the pages of this book create an opening in the hearts of all of those who read these words, so that there is no doubt that there is only One—that all is Divine. Wherever there is life, there is an outpicturing of Father/Mother God—from whatever planet, whatever Universe, whatever star system, from the Earth and all her Kingdoms—the stone people, the animals, the plants, the trees, those in the center of the Earth—KNOW that all life is part of the Law of One.

The attempts by the Illuminati to implant fear and hostility into the hearts and minds of our children and our people through movies, games, the media by saying that the "space beings" are coming to destroy us and that we are the "only intelligence and the only planet where life can be sustained" is the height of spiritual arrogance!

Where would we have been without the sustained protection of the Ashtar Command those many eons before the Harmonic Convergence and since? I just read in my notes a channeling from Ashtar years ago that life on this planet could not have been sustained beyond 2003 had not it been for the ships stabilizing the planet and keeping it from turning over on its axis. How would the oil spill that had already made its way into the aquifers in the Gulf of Mexico been cleaned up so quickly without the enzymes provided by the ships . . . and what of the earthquakes that caused no tsunamis and the deadly storms that were dissipated or redirected and on and on and on?

We all need to say a prayer of thanksgiving every day to the ships in the Ashtar Command that protect this planet.

Along the path to everywhere
The tensile strength upholds the beam
Across the never ending distance
To places long unseen.
It brings along the path courage, strength and inner sight.
To those who ask its blessing—it showers out the Light.
From in the strong connection to all the past and yet to be
Ever moving, ever loving—
The protection of eternity.

Joyce Strahn

I am ready to begin the transmission:
Good. We are here.

This day is the turning point in the consciousness of man. What was started with the Harmonic Convergence takes on new meaning today as millions worldwide turn their attention to the Goddess and see the devastation that they have created on the planet. From this time forth, a new awareness will be created and no person will be quite as deluded as in the past. The life of the Mother is the life of humankind. One cannot die without the death of the other. Awareness is the key to survival, and change will be made.

Illness is rampant on the land. Little ones suffer as an example that ones may see they (the children) have not created the devastation, yet they give their lives. Because of the greed of man whose emphasis has been on survival, with money being what he considers a necessity for survival, the loss of jobs is where he has placed his energy. Man is beginning to see more than his shortsighted vision has beheld before, that the consequences of imbalance are disease and death, and only through wholeness and balance will all be restored to rightness.

As the energy of love is imbued into each part of the planet, each leaf, each grain of sand, each simple garden spot, each flower, each forest, each stream, and as man learns to give thanks for the abundance that has been always a part of his incarnation, the planet will respond in the joy of being heard and the little ones will burst forth to rekindle the Light on the Earth which gives life to all.

Oh, ye who are once heralds of the Kingdom of Light on Earth, give of yourselves freely in this time. Speak your truth without reservation. Show by your example the urgency of the issues at hand. Allow the love of your hearts and the energy from your bodies and your hands to heal everything you touch. As you greet each day and each moment with all of your love energy, coming in complete gratitude for the life that flows within you, acknowledge your connection with the ONE POWER, the God within. There will be time to rescue this planet and create a heaven on Earth. The masses will turn about in wrath from the destruction at hand. Nature will sweep with wind and water across the land and bring forth a great garden of lushness and life more abundant than anything ever before seen on the Earth. Flowers will bloom where never before there was life, crops will grow that never before were known in the land, and food will be created out of nothingness.

Have no fear. Be only in love. Allow the God-force to breathe you. Feel the column of energy rise up within you. Feel the swirling energies about your heads and KNOW we are one with thee. Through your gift of willingness to be in Truth and Joy, we can work miracles on the planet. Time will move swiftly to a conclusion. Ones willing to love and share their love with others will survive. Ones who are Intent on destruction will be borne away. Rejoice, dear ones, the time is at hand. It begins now. Fear no more. The ball rolls with the mass of consciousness ever larger, ever stronger. In the next days and weeks, practices that rape the land will be stopped, the air will clear, health will come again to the masses. You will see it will come quickly. Go in grace and willingness to obey the commands of your higher selves. Work. Listen. Obey. The time is at hand.

A time of great change is upon the Earth. We emerge from a war greater than your World Wars. It is a War of the Spirit . . . it is a rebirth into the consciousness of the God-self into human expression. Your first task is to learn to deal with the new energies being given to Earth. These energies can either be a blessing or a deterrent. Rise up into the new thoughts and feelings of love that come into your minds. Hang not onto the old ways. Let the ego crumble and burn away. Its function is outmoded and outdated now. Join your higher consciousness with the Universal consciousness and make the merging a permanent infiltration of your energy system. Act as though you are a god, for you are. Be aware that as you speak and think, it shall be done. Know that if you act or think or have Intent to harm any of God's creations, you will be destroyed. This is what is meant by the narrow way. Only as you love and seek to aid man and animals and Nature, will you grow and expand in your growth.

Ones from the ships have for some time now been monitoring the Earth and holding her in position until Earth's people could, through their own doing, balance the negative energies she has been immersed in for so long. The energy streams we have poured out upon the Earth have bombarded the consciousness of the sleeping ones and, those who would hear, have begun to awaken. Many will never awaken from the sleep of death.

For thousands of years, you have been told that changes would come on this planet, yet you heeded not. Many of our strongest souls have been sent and even they, though they did their best, have made but a small dent in the minds of men. You are so deluded by your belief that material things are your gods, that money and power are all that matters. You seek God in places called religions that have become but shallow remnants of a once powerful connection between God and man. Into this mock structure filled with the egos of men, you place your faith that should be given to God alone. You accept the words from the mouths of men filled with power and their own sense of justice, instead of realizing that you need not their speeches and pretty words. Even their Intent has gone astray. Very few have yet the humility and the courage to remain connected to the Source.

It is now time to begin anew. The message of the NEW AGE is Peace on Earth. Gently it must come into the hearts of men as it began 2000 years ago. Gently it must permeate the consciousness of all men everywhere. Raise not your voice or your hand against your brother, but neither allow another to take over your own power and control, for you are the supreme commander of your own being and your own soul. Allow the voice that speaks within to be the loudest voice. Listen and be still. Hear its voice.

As the rain gently permeates the Earth, so shall the thoughts of men be permeated with thoughts of good and healing for others. Through man's caring the Earth is healed. Through man's cooperation with the Kingdoms of God, all will be made right upon the planet. Be not afraid to speak out. Be not afraid to make change.

I AM Ashtar. I AM Sananda. We are the Ashtar Command. Namaste!

CPSIA information can be obtained at www.ICGtesting.com
Printed in the USA
BVOW041615190412

288110BV00001B/11/P